JOHN
IN THE NOW

THE GOSPEL OF ST. JOHN
RE-IMAGINED IN MODERN CONTEXT

BISHOP JIM SWILLEY

JOHN IN THE NOW, The Gospel of St. John Re-Imagined in Modern Context
ISBN 978-0-9787170-0-1
Copyright © 2006 by Jim Swilley

Published by Church In The Now Publishing
1877 Iris Drive, SE
Conyers, GA 30013

Cover design by A-Grafixx Design Group, www.agrafixx.com

Foreword

Why write a new paraphrase of the book of John?

1. Because I love Jesus. I love the *real,* living Jesus...the outspoken, passionate, confrontational, provocative, liberating, counter-culture, strong and brave and totally secure-within-Himself, fully integrated Jesus...the Word made flesh who became Jesus, the Christ...Jesus in the now...the One who embodies the "I AM," the God who defies definition and description...the manna or the "what is it?" that came down from heaven...the One whose humanity is every bit as beautiful and intriguing and wonderful as is His divinity...the God-man who cannot be bound or limited in any way by religion or philosophy or doctrines or dogma...the firstborn among many siblings in the family of God who live in the 21st century. I love that real Jesus now more than ever and am in no way offended that He says that I must eat His flesh and drink His blood to have a revelation of Him!

2. Because I love the Scriptures. They are a part of me, as absorbed into the fiber of my being as they could possibly be. The words of God vibrate in every cell of my body...they occupy the largest part of my mind...they completely saturate my spirit. The Bible is a miracle – **not a book,** but a collection of 66 books written by 40 authors over a period of 1,500 years in different languages to different people groups in different generations for different purposes. Therefore, the Scriptures must be *rightly divided* instead of *wrongly connected.* In other words, each book must be judged in its own context and on its own terms, whether it confirms any other book or not. In this way, biblical contradictions are not only acknowledged and accepted, but they are expected. I celebrate the tension caused by the conflicting viewpoints of the writers who had different paradigms of God; their contradictions make the Bible literally pulsate with life! And amazingly, in spite of the given contention, the confirmation of Jesus, the Christ, is still the glue that holds the whole collection together!

3. Because I love the Gospel of John. John's gospel is unique – so different from the three synoptic gospels of Matthew, Mark and Luke. They are all certainly wonderful biographies of the God-man, and each one brings something original to the table, but John's account of the greatest story ever told is in a class all by itself. It is the gospel written for non-conformists and individualists – for those who can comprehend Jesus outside the box. Can you imagine the visionary mind of someone who begins his story with, *"In the beginning was the Word, and the Word was with God, and the Word was God"*? You could spend a lifetime just discussing that one wonderful sentence and still would not be able to fully plumb the depths of its meaning!

4. Because I love the diversity among all the translations and paraphrases of the Bible. Although I wholeheartedly reject the notion of an official "authorized version," I do honor the grandeur and loftiness of the Bible that James, the King of England, authorized for his subjects to read in the 17th century (*King James Version*). That's why I have memorized vast sections of it. And I love the way James Moffatt could turn a phrase in his translation. I could virtually live in *The Amplified Bible* with all of its shades of meanings and wordy explanations and parentheses and brackets. It's like heaven to someone who loves exploring words and their meanings as I do. When I was young, Kenneth Taylor's beautifully accessible *Living Bible* changed my life and set the course for my whole ministry. Many years later, Eugene Peterson's daring paraphrase called *The Message* affected me nearly as dramatically. In recent years I have grown to respect the *Today's New International Version* for its modernity and clarity and lack of religious sexism. In my opinion, it is probably the most accurate of them all. But I also love the *New English Bible* and *The Jerusalem Bible* for other reasons. I am constantly referring to all of these translations for my teaching and writing, along with some other great ones not mentioned here. You may ask then, "If you love all these translations so much, why write a new one?" My only answer is that this writing is my way to pay homage to those who have already blazed this trail of translation before me. I could not do this if they hadn't done what they did. But this translation is what *I* hear when I read and teach these chapters and verses. These are the things *I* have seen...what *I* have read between the lines...for the last 35 years of ministry, and I simply submit them to you, the reader, for your consideration.

5. Because I love communication. Nothing is more important to the life of relationships than communication, and nothing is more gratifying than knowing that you have effectively communicated your message to someone else. I certainly don't claim to know everything about Jesus; in fact, the more that I increase in my knowledge of Him throughout the course of my life, the more mysterious He actually becomes to me. For me that's not a problem. I'm rather glad that, even though I know Him more intimately than I know anyone else, there is always a part of Him that is past my finding out. I know that I will never reach the limits of the breadth and length and depth and height of Him, ever. But, what I do know about Him is the most wonderful knowledge that I possess, and I have a need to share that knowledge with others.

6. Because I love people. One of the greatest songs ever written contains the words, *"If I can help somebody as I pass along...then my living shall not be in vain."* I try to live by the philosophy of that song, so if this book can help someone to rediscover and rethink the Bible – someone who has previously been intimidated or confused or bored by it, regardless of its available translations and paraphrases –

then I will have fulfilled at least a part of my destiny. I want to help people know and love Jesus better, but I also want to make them more comfortable with the Bible and with their own interpretations and opinions about it. The Bible is hearty, robust – it is not delicate or fragile – it can withstand a lot of handling by human beings because it was meant to be people-friendly, and I want to open a door to the house of understanding and let the people in!

7. Because I love living in the now. More than anything else, I believe that I was specifically put here on this planet to be a good steward of the concept of living in the now. God is in the now because He is always revealed as the I AM. His word is in the now because people cannot live on bread alone, but on every word that proceeds (present tense) out of His mouth. His kingdom is in the now because it can only be discerned one day at a time by those who take no thought for tomorrow. I will proclaim and defend the doctrine of the "now-ness" of God for as long as I live and will aggressively wage war on every religious idea that tries to relegate God to the past or attempts to project Him into the future. God is always now and my prayer is that, as you read *John In The Now,* you will walk in a full revelation of that. Now is all that matters!

Bishop Jim Swilley

Introduction

Many ancient biographies were written about Jesus, but only the four that we call The Gospels are included in the traditional Christian canon. A very popular notion among some theologians over the years has been to liken the distinct personalities of these four Gospels to the four living creatures that Ezekiel saw in the spirit, and I think that is an interesting way to observe the similarities and diversity found in each of them:

"...and in the fire was what looked like four living creatures. In appearance their form was human, but each of them had four faces and four wings. Their faces looked like this:

Each of the four had the face of a *human being*
(Luke, presenting Jesus as the Perfect Man),

and on the right side each had the face of a *lion*
(Matthew, presenting Jesus as a Great King),

and on the left the face of an *ox*
(Mark, presenting Jesus as a True Servant);

each also had the face of an *eagle.* "
(John, presenting Jesus as The Mighty God made flesh).

– Ezekiel 1:5, 6, 10 - TNIV

The Gospel of Matthew embraces a certain paradigm because it was written primarily to the Jews. It employs the writing style of that of a teacher, emphasizes Jesus' sermons, and contains a genealogical record because a **king** must have one (it traces the regal line of David through his son Solomon, and leads to Joseph, the legal stepfather of Jesus). The Gospel of

Mark derives its particular tone from having been written to the Romans. It's writing style embodies the perspective of a preacher, and it emphasizes Jesus' miracles. It does not contain His genealogical record because a **servant** doesn't need one. The Gospel of Luke was originally combined with the Book of Acts and was written to the Greeks. It's writing style is one that would typically belong to a historian. It emphasizes the parables of Jesus and does contain His genealogical record because a perfect **man** should have one (it traces the physical line of David through another son, Nathan, and leads to Mary, the physical mother of Jesus).

But John's account of the Jesus story is not written to any particular people group, as are the Synoptic Gospels; it is written to the whole world. It's writing style is really that of a theologian, and it emphasizes the doctrines of Christ. But it does not contain a genealogical record of Him, because **God** doesn't have one – God is always *now*. Both Matthew and Luke begin their stories in Bethlehem, while John chooses to originate his gospel *in the beginning*. As the eagle flies above the weather, the Gospel of John rises above predictability and sameness. All of the drama in Matthew, Mark and Luke unfolds in Capernaum in Galilee, while John centers the action of his version all around the metropolitan community of Jerusalem in Judea.

Interesting Facts

There are only seven incidents recorded in the Gospel of John that can be found in the other gospels: John's word, the Last Supper, the anointing at Bethany, the feeding of the 5,000, the walking on the sea, the Passion and the Resurrection. All other events mentioned in the fourth gospel are peculiar to John.

The number seven seems to figure quite prominently throughout John:

Seven witnesses of Jesus, the Christ:

1. John the Baptist (1:34)
2. Nathanael (1:49)
3. Samaritan woman (4:29)
4. Peter (6:69)
5. Martha (11:27)
6. Thomas (20:28)
7. John the Apostle (21:7)

Seven pre-crucifixion miracles:

1. Water into wine (2:1-11)
2. Healing of the nobleman's son (4:46-54)
3. Healing of a man at the Pool of Bethesda (5:1-47)
4. Feeding of the 5,000 (6:1-14)
5. Walking on the water (6:15-21)
6. Healing of the man born blind (9:1-41)
7. Raising of Lazarus (11:1-57)

Seven I Am's:

1. I am the bread of life (6:35)
2. I am the light (8:12)
3. I am in the now ("Before Abraham was, I AM") (8:58)
4. I am the good shepherd (10:11)
5. I am the resurrection (11:25)
6. I am the way, the truth, and the life (14:6)
7. I am the true vine (15:1)

Authorship

John was the son of Zebedee and the brother of James, the apostle. His mother, Salome, was the sister of Mary, the mother of Jesus, so he was actually Jesus' first cousin. The family lived in Galilee, probably at Bethsaida, where Zebedee and his two sons were fishermen on the Sea of Galilee. It would seem that John's family was not without some means, because they had hired servants, which means that they belonged to the employer class. Luke 8:3 and Mark 15:40 reveal that Salome was one of the women who ministered to Jesus out of their own prosperity and was also one of the women who brought spices and came to anoint His body at the tomb (Mark 16:11). John seems to be referring to himself as the disciple in Chapter 18 of his gospel, and the fact that he knew the high priest well enough to gain entrance to the court where Jesus was tried and could get permission for Peter to enter, would also suggest that his family was not exactly poor.

He refers to himself in the story in the first person, introducing himself initially as a disciple of John the Baptist, who then repented and followed Jesus. No one knew Jesus better than John. Not only were they related, but they walked together from day to day as close, personal friends. John physically leaned on Him at the Last Supper, stood by His cross, was entrusted with the care of His mother, entered His tomb, and freely referred to himself as that disciple that Jesus loved. He wrote his gospel around the same time that he wrote his three epistles (90 A.D.), which was about six years before he wrote the Revelation of Jesus Christ on the Isle of Patmos. Tradition says that he penned the gospel in Asia at the request of Christian friends who wanted to preserve his first-hand account of the earth-life of Jesus, and that he agreed to do so only after the church had fasted and prayed about the matter for three days. He spent his last years in Ephesus, and apparently died there about the end of the century.

JOHN

IN THE NOW

THE GOSPEL OF ST. JOHN

RE-IMAGINED IN MODERN CONTEXT

Chapter 1

1. In the beginning, or in the eternal "now" before the creation of time, was the Word...the Logos...the Christ. And that timeless Christ/Word existed with God and, in fact, that Word actually was God, Himself.

2. He was originally omnipresent with God.

3. All things in the realm of space and time came into existence through the specific expression of that "now" Word, and without the expression of that Word was not even one thing made that has come into being in the material universe.

4. In His being was housed the source of life, and that life was the light that illuminates all of humanity.

5. And the light shines on in the darkness, for darkness has never been able to absorb the light, nor will it ever be able to overpower it or put it out.

6. There was a man who was God-sent, and his name was John.

7. John came to bear witness of the Light that everyone, everywhere, might believe in it through him.

8. He was not the Light, but came that he might verify the truth that is in the Light.

9. And there it was, the true Light, coming in perfection to illuminate every individual on the planet.

10. He came into the world that He, Himself, had created, but that same world did not recognize Him, initially.

11. He appeared to that which already belonged to Him; He entered into His own domain and creation. But that creation did not welcome or receive Him.

12. Yet, to all who did receive and welcome Him by believing in the power of His name, He granted the authority to walk in the full reality that they were the children of God...

13. children born divinely of God...not merely of natural descent nor of human decision or will.

14. And the eternal Word morphed into flesh – into a manifested incarnation with human attributes and authority in the natural world – so that He could live with and among us human beings. And He did live with us here in our world, limiting Himself to the constraints of the human condition without reservation, but we could still plainly see His eternal, divine glory. It was obvious that He shined with the glorious light of a unique, firstborn son who was miraculously like His Father who had sent Him. The illumination from that glory revealed that He was literally filled with grace and that He overflowed with absolute truth.

15. John identified Him by boldly and publicly declaring, "This is the One! This is the One who I said was coming after me! But, in reality, He was and is actually *before* me – He already existed in the now – and that is why He is superior to me!

16. "For out of the flow of His fullness we have all received gift after gift, grace upon grace, one spiritual blessing after another, favor heaped upon favor.

17. "For while the limited and limiting law was laid down by Moses, amazing grace – undeserved, unmerited, unearned, *un*limited – along with the full revelation of the truth which has freely appeared to everyone, came through Jesus, the Christ.

18. "No one in this realm has ever really seen God in His fullness, but the unique Son, who is Himself God and is in closest relationship with and to the Father, has revealed Him and has made Him known to us."

19. And this was John's testimony when the Jews sent priests and Levites to him from Jerusalem to ask him, "Who are you?"

20. He was quick to confess to them that he, by himself, was not the Christ.

21. They asked him, "Then who are you? Are you the reincarnation of Elijah?" He said, "No, I am not."

Then they asked, "Are you the Prophet?" He answered, "No."

22. Finally they said, "Well, then, who are you? Answer us so that we can answer those who sent us to you. What do you say about yourself and your mission?"

23. He answered them by paraphrasing the words of the prophet Isaiah, saying, "I am essentially nothing more than a voice...the voice of one crying in the wilderness or shouting out in the desert...to prepare the way of the Lord!"

24. The messengers had been sent from the Pharisees,

25. and they asked him, "Why, then, are you baptizing people if you are not the Christ, or Elijah reincarnated, or the Prophet? What is the point that you are trying to make?"

26. John answered them, "I only baptize by using the familiar and recognizable symbolism of water, but One stands among you whom you do not recognize and with whom you are not familiar – and His baptism will change everything.

27. "He is the One who comes after me in the realm of time, the thongs of whose sandals I am not worthy to untie."

28. These conversations took place in Bethany, at the Jordan crossing where John was then baptizing.

29. The next day, John saw Jesus coming toward him and cried out, "See, recognize, discern and perceive the Lamb of God who takes away the sin of the whole world!

30. "This is He of whom I said would come after me in *time*, but is actually superior to me because He existed, as He is, in the *now*. He was before me because He *is* before me.

31. "I myself did not recognize Him at first, but now that I can see who He is, I am baptizing with water as a means to reveal Him to the nation of Israel."

32. Then John went on to say, "I saw the Spirit come

from the eternal realm, like a dove that appeared to fly down out of the limitless sky and light on Him. And it, or He, remained on Him and filled Him, making His home in Him.

33. "And that is how I recognized Him, because the One who sent me to baptize with water said to me, 'The man on whom you see the Spirit come down and remain is He who will baptize with the Holy Spirit.'

34. "And so I confidently make this testimony because there is no doubt in my mind that He is the Son of God."

35. Again the next day, John was in the same place with two of his followers,

36. and he looked at Jesus walking along and said to them, "Look at Him! He is the Lamb of God!"

37. When the two disciples of John heard this, they were so impacted by it that they immediately stopped following John and began to follow Jesus.

38. Jesus, aware that they were following Him, turned around and asked, "What do you want?" They said, "Teacher, we want to see where You live, or at least where You are staying; we want to go to Your house."

39. "Come," He replied, "and you will see." So they went to His house and spent the whole day with Him. It was about four in the afternoon.

40. Andrew (Simon Peter's brother) was one of the two who had followed Jesus after hearing John's words.

41. Immediately after visiting Jesus' house, Andrew found his brother Simon and told him, "We have found the Christ – the One anointed to be the Messiah!"

42. And he brought him to Jesus, who took one look at him and said, prophetically, "You see yourself simply as Simon, the son of John, but I see that you are a foundation stone, so I am calling you Cephas, which is translated Peter, 'the Rock.'"

43. The next day Jesus decided to travel to Galilee. There He found Philip and He said to him, "I want you to follow Me."

44. Philip had a connection with Andrew and Peter, because they were all from the town of Bethsaida.

45. Philip then found Nathanael and told him, "We have found the One that Moses wrote about in the law – the One about whom the prophets also wrote – and He is Jesus of Nazareth, the legal son of Joseph, the carpenter!"

46. "Nazareth!" Nathanael exclaimed. "Has anything good ever come from there or *can* anything good ever come from there?" Philip said, "You need to come and see it for yourself."

47. When Jesus saw Nathanael approaching, He said of him, "Look at that! An authentic Israelite indeed, in whom there is no guile, falsehood or pretense."

48. Nathanael asked, "How do You know me, the *real* me?" Jesus answered, "Before Philip ever called you, I saw you. You were under a fig tree and I could see you right there where you were standing."

49. Then Nathanael, remembering that he was, indeed, standing under a fig tree right before Philip had approached him, declared, "Teacher, You are the Son of God! And I say that You are the King of Israel!"

50. Jesus said, "You believe because I told you that I saw you under the fig tree, but let Me tell you, you will see greater things than that!"

51. Then He said to him, "I'm telling you the truth – all of you – that the eternal or heavenly realm is about to be completely opened up, and the angels of God will interact with the Son of Man by ascending and descending upon Him, and you will see it all in the now!"

Chapter 2

1. On the third day, a wedding took place at Cana of Galilee, and Mary (Jesus' mother) was there.

2. And Jesus was also invited to the wedding, along with His newly chosen disciples.

3. At a certain point in the celebration, Mary came to Jesus and said to Him, pointedly, "You should know that the hosts of this reception have no more wine to serve their guests, and there is no place for the caterers to get more."

4. Jesus replied, "That really is none of our business, Mother, so why are you telling Me? Don't try to draw Me into a natural situation in an attempt to push Me into doing the supernatural. I will not perform a miracle prematurely or before My time."

5. Mary, completely ignoring Jesus' words of protest, turned to the caterers and said, "Just do whatever He tells you to do."

6. Now there were six stone water jars right there in front of Him (the kind used by the Jews for ceremonial washing), each holding twenty to thirty gallons.

7. So Jesus said to the servants, "Very well, then…fill up these big vessels with water." So they filled them all the way to the brim.

8. Then He said to them, "Now take a sample to the host of the banquet."

9. When the host tasted the water transformed into wine, he called the bridegroom aside and said, "I don't know where you've been keeping all of this very fine wine, but it is exquisite!

10. "And what impresses me is that, usually, at these events the people who hire me want me to serve the choice wine first and then the cheaper stuff after the guests have had too much to drink and don't notice or

care. But you have the class and good taste to save the best until now!"

11.	And this miraculous sign (that Jesus was more or less forced into performing) was the first among many of His wonders and, as a result, His disciples put their faith in Him, without reservation.

12.	After this He went down to Capernaum with His mother and brothers and His disciples, and they spent several days together there.

13.	When it was almost time for Passover, Jesus traveled to Jerusalem.

14.	Upon entering the temple courts there, He became enraged with what He saw going on inside. It looked more like an out-of-control stock market than a temple, with people all over the place selling cattle, sheep and doves. And in the middle of it all was an operation of loan sharks and money exchangers loudly doing business.

15.	So, transferring His righteous anger into action, He took disciplinary matters into His own hands and fashioned out a whip of many leather cords. Then He took the whip and actually began chasing the business owners around, threatening them with it. He drove them all from the temple courts and then scattered the coinage of the moneychangers by violently flipping over the tables they had set up for their transactions.

16.	As He ran after them He shouted, "Get all of this garbage out of here and stop turning My Father's beautiful house into an ugly place of shady commerce!"

17.	The scenario caused His disciples to remember that it is written in the Psalms, "The zeal for your house will literally consume me!"

18.	Then the people there in Jerusalem challenged Him, saying, "Show us a sign to validate Your authority to do such a thing! Who do You think You are, and why do You presume to be in charge of the temple operation?"

19. Jesus answered them, "If you want a sign, then destroy this temple and I will raise it up again in three days!"

20. They replied, "Are You serious? It has taken forty-six years to build this temple and You think that You can rebuild it in three days?"

21. What they didn't realize was that Jesus, speaking prophetically, was changing the whole concept and paradigm of the temple. On one level He was answering them about the temple as they saw it, but He was actually referring to the temple of His own body that would be raised back to life after being dead for three days.

22. After the resurrection, His disciples recalled what He had said that day. And it really wasn't until then that they believed that His words had fulfilled the Scriptures.

23. Now while He was in Jerusalem at the Passover Feast, many people saw His miraculous signs and entrusted their lives to Him.

24. But Jesus would not entrust Himself to them, for He really knew people – all people – on a deep, personal level.

25. He did not need anyone's explanation or warning about humanity, for He Himself was more than just perceptive and intuitive. He could actually read the hearts of people and could discern – even empathize with – all of the complexities of human nature, including its dark side.

Chapter 3

1. Now there was a man named Nicodemus who was a Pharisee, a member of the Jewish ruling council.

2. He secretly approached Jesus under the cover of night

and said to Him, "Rabbi, it is obvious to all of us that You are a God-sent, God-ordained teacher, for no one could perform the amazing signs You are doing if God were not with him."

3. Jesus replied, "*This* is what is important – even more important than the signs – *this* truth is absolute: No one can perceive the concept of the kingdom of God without experiencing a rebirth of sorts...without having actually revisited the human birth process."

4. "What are You talking about?" Nicodemus asked. "How could any adult be born *again*? They obviously couldn't return to the womb, so how could *rebirth* possibly happen?"

5. Jesus answered, "I'm telling you, unreservedly, that no one can access the kingdom of God unless they are first physically born of water (the natural birth that begins when a pregnant woman's water breaks) and then have their thought processes *reborn* by having them washed with the *water* of the Word, which is the result of the birth of the Spirit.

6. "Every living thing in the physical realm gives birth to, or recreates, a physical manifestation, and everything spiritual gives birth to a spiritual reality. Whatever is birthed from the Spirit is the essence of spirit.

7. "Look, you shouldn't be so surprised to hear Me say 'You must be born again.'

8. "Think of it this way: the wind blows wherever it wants to blow...it has a mind of its own. You can hear it, but you can't locate its place of origin and you can't predict its destination. This is how it is with everyone who is birthed out of the Spirit-wind."

9. Nicodemus said, "I don't understand. What exactly are You talking about?"

10. Jesus said to him, "How can you be such a great teacher of truth – one who deals with abstract thought...one of the greatest in Israel, in fact – and not

be able to grasp this concept?

11. "Here's the truth: I only speak of what I know by experience and verify what I have seen with My own eyes. My revelation is organic. But you who are overly-educated and pretentiously religious do not accept My testimony.

12. "If I have told you of things that happen right here in the finite, earthly realm and none of you believes Me, how can you possibly comprehend My description of the infinite...the eternal things that are in the now?

13. "No one has ever gone into the eternal realm called heaven except the One who came from there, namely, the Son of Man.

14. "And just as Moses lifted up the snake in the wilderness for all to see, so the Son of Man must be lifted up in the same way,

15. so that everyone who believes in Him may walk in the fullness of their eternal life.

16. "You see, God's love for the whole world – His paternal affection for the entire cosmos – was so all-encompassing and complete that He freely gave His unique Son to it, so that anyone from that world who believes in Him would not perish, but would awaken to the fact that eternal life is theirs.

17. "It certainly was never God's intention to send His Son into the world to pronounce a sentence of condemnation upon it. Rather, He was perfectly focused on saving it...on redeeming the whole of humanity...everyone and everything on the planet...through the gift of that unique, manifested Son.

18. "Those who believe in the Son never come up for judgment because their faith causes them to be acquitted. Those who do not believe live their lives as though they were under a death sentence, because they do not embrace a faith in the name of the unique Son of God.

19. "The bottom line is this: Light has come into the world, but people loved darkness instead of light because their deeds were evil.

20. "Those who ignorantly practice evil hate the Light and will not come into it because they fear that the Light will expose them and their deeds.

21. "But those who desire to live truthfully come into the light with no fear. They welcome the Light and are not afraid for the Light to reveal who they really are."

22. After this, Jesus and His disciples went out into the countryside of Judea to spend some bonding time together, and Jesus also baptized some people there.

23. But John was also baptizing at Aenon near Salim, because there was a lot of water there and people kept coming to him to be baptized.

24. This was before John was thrown into prison and everything was still good between him and Jesus.

25. And an argument developed between some of John's disciples and a local Jewish man over the matter of ceremonial washing.

26. And they approached John and said to him, "Teacher, the man who was with you on the other side of the Jordan – the One that you've been talking about so much – is also baptizing, and everyone seems to be going to Him instead of you."

27. And John replied, "A spiritual man can receive nothing except it has been granted to him from the spirit-realm. By that, I mean he must be content to receive the gift that has been given him from heaven because there really is no other source for gifts.

28. "And you yourselves know that I have freely admitted that I, alone, am not the Christ and that I have not been anointed to be the Messiah. My mission is simply to be His forerunner and to prepare the world for His reign.

29. "The bride belongs to the bridegroom. The bridegroom's 'best man' at the wedding listens for

him and waits on him; in fact, he is full of joy for his friend's happiness. And so, if you follow my analogy, you should know my joy is now full. I am happy to have been a part of the wedding ceremony, but I know that I am only the 'best man,' as it were.

30. "What I am saying is that, even though I have fulfilled my destiny in this respect, His influence must become greater now. The attention needs to be more on Him and less on me, from this point on.

31. "The One who comes from the now, or the eternal, heavenly realm (or from what you perceive as *above*), is, in fact, above all. Whoever is from the earth belongs to the earth, speaks the language of the earth, is limited to earthly constraints of space and time, and speaks entirely from an earthly paradigm. The One from heaven is transcendent.

32. "It is the One from heaven who relays what He has seen and heard *in the now*, but no one limited by the material world accepts His testimony.

33. "The individual who has accepted it, however, has certified and declared, once and for all, that God is absolutely real and His words are completely true.

34. "For the One whom God has sent speaks the words of God, for God gives Him His Spirit without measure or the limits of time or space. He holds within Himself the infinite universe of the Spirit.

35. "The Father loves the Son and has placed everything in His hands, committing all things to His dominion.

36. "And he or she who believes in the Son by perceiving who He is, understands the reality of his or her eternal life. But whoever does not believe in the Son does not enjoy the benefits of eternal life, but lives as though the wrath of God were hanging over him or her, continually."

Chapter 4

1. When Jesus became aware that the Pharisees had heard that He was gaining and baptizing more disciples than John, He realized that they were trying to turn John and Him into rivals in the eyes of the people.

2. (For what it's worth, Jesus didn't actually baptize the people...His disciples did.)

3. So He left Judea and went back again to Galilee.

4. Now He had to go through Samaria to get there.

5. And He came to a town in that country called Sychar, near the plot of ground that Jacob had bequeathed to his son Joseph.

6. The famous and historical "Jacob's Well" was there and, because everyone who lived in the village had to get their water from that location, it also served as the hub and focal point of all the town's communication and social life.

7. When He saw a certain anonymous Samaritan woman come to draw water from the well, Jesus said to her, "Excuse Me, but will you please give Me a drink?"

8. He was sitting there alone because His disciples had gone into the town to buy food.

9. The Samaritan woman replied, "Mister, do You realize how many things are wrong with the statement You just made? You are a Jew. I am a Samaritan. You are a man. I am a woman. And You are a *stranger*, no less, so how is it that You think You can ask me for a drink, especially since Jews have nothing to do with Samaritans?"

10. Jesus answered her, "Listen, if you could discern the gift of God...if you could comprehend who it is that asks you for a drink...you would have seized the opportunity to ask *Him* and He would have given you water that is literally alive and life-giving."

11. The woman said to Him, "Is that so? Well, You have no bucket to draw with and the well is very deep, so how can You get to Your so-called 'living water'?

12. "Do You presume to be greater than our father Jacob...the one who really made this well live? His well has been sustaining life for generations, just like it did for his own sons and flocks and herds."

13. Jesus answered, "Everyone who drinks the water from this well will be thirsty again,

14. but those who drink the water that I have to give will never experience thirst...ever! See, I am actually able to tap into a spring of life-giving water from within a person. In the same way that Jacob put this well here in Sychar, I can locate and dig an artesian well within your spirit and mind that will become a constant source of eternal life for you!"

15. Intrigued with this mysterious stranger and His unusual proposition, she said, "Sir, give me this water so that I won't get thirsty and have to come here every morning to get my water for the day."

16. He said to her, "All right, but I want you to go and get your husband and bring him back with you, and then I'll tell you more about it."

17. "Well," she said, "The thing is...I don't have a husband." Jesus said to her, "I'm glad that you admitted that you have no husband,

18. because the truth is that you have actually had five husbands in all, and the man that you're currently living with as your husband is not even married to you. You have very readily and succinctly spoken the truth about yourself."

19. "How could You possibly know that?" she asked in astonishment. "You must truly be a prophet!"

20. "Let me ask You something: our ancestors worshipped on this mountain, but you Jews claim that the place where we must worship is in Jerusalem."

21. "Lady," Jesus replied, "believe Me when I tell you that a time is coming when you will worship the Father neither on this mountain nor in Jerusalem.

22. "The truth is, you Samaritans are basically clueless about worship. We Jews do understand the dynamics of it, for salvation, before becoming universal, is going to originate in Israel through the Jews. But there is another and greater dimension of worship that is opening up...one that transcends nationality or ethnicity or religion or ancestry.

23. "In fact, you may find this hard to believe because of your past and present lifestyle, but the Father is actually looking for worshippers just like you...people who are candid and honest about their lives and histories, without making any bogus attempt to justify themselves. Transparent people like you – no matter where you have come from or how many failed marriages you've had – who are able to worship in the Spirit, regardless of the truth about themselves.

24. "And the reason is that *God is spirit* and His worshippers must worship Him *in the Spirit*, which means that they must worship Him truthfully, honestly, with the same candor that you demonstrated in being honest about your life. Worship in the Spirit requires that you free yourself of the façade of flesh...that the real you worships the real God."

25. The woman said, "I don't know about all that, but I do know that the Messiah, or the Christ, is coming, and when He comes He will explain God and the realities of the spirit world to us."

26. Then Jesus said to her, "Isn't it obvious to you, yet? I, the One sitting here at this well talking to you about all this, am He! I am the One you've really been looking for all these years, and I can supply you with something superior to anything any of these other men in your life could ever give you."

27. While He was speaking these words, His disciples returned and were, frankly, surprised to find Him just blatantly ignoring propriety and the cultural mores of the day by talking so freely with a strange, native woman of Samaria…one who could, most likely, be another man's wife…right out in the open like that. But no one made it their business to ask Him anything about it.

28. Then suddenly, leaving her water jar there, the woman jumped up from where she had been sitting and talking with Jesus, headed back to town, and started telling everyone that she could find about what had just taken place.

29. She said to anyone who would listen, "You've got to come meet this man that I just met at the well! He is definitely a prophet because He told me everything that I ever did. But He is more than a prophet. In fact, He says He is the Messiah and I think that He just might be!"

30. She was so convincing…her testimony so compelling…that the people from town just started following her back to where she had left Jesus, and some even made their own way to meet Him for themselves.

31. As they began to flock to Him, His disciples said, "Teacher, a crowd is forming to hear from You, but before You minister to them You should eat something."

32. But He said to them, "I appreciate your concern for Me, but you should know that what sustains Me…what satisfies My hunger…is something you know nothing about, yet."

33. So His disciples, missing the point, asked Him if someone had already brought Him something to eat.

34. Jesus said to them, "My nourishment comes from doing the will of Him who sent Me and to finish His work. Whether it's one-on-one, as with this woman

at the well, or ministering to this gathering crowd, this is what feeds and sustains Me!

35. "Stop limiting your concept of food to the natural. Do you not say, 'It is still four months until harvest time comes?' Well, I'm talking about the harvest of spiritual produce...a crop in the now. Lift up your eyes and look at these fields right now! These people here are the field...our field of harvest...and the harvest is ripe right now!

36. "Already the reaper is getting his wages. The one who does the harvesting has his reward *now*, for he is gathering a crop of eternal lives. And the one who does the planting rejoices with one who picks the crop, because it all happens – sowing *and* reaping – together *in the now*!

37. "For in this the saying holds true about the synergy of harvesting: one sows and another reaps, and together they produce what neither could produce individually.

38. "I have sent you to reap a crop for which you have not labored. Others, like the prophets and those who have preached about the coming Messiah, have toiled in the field, and you are able to step in to reap the results of their work."

39. By this time many Samaritans from the town began to believe in Him, mainly because of the power of the testimony of this woman who said, "This man told me everything I ever did." She obviously seemed to be amazed by His prophetic ability, but what really impressed them is that she didn't appear to be put off at all by a Jewish stranger so matter-of-factly reading her mail, so to speak. On the contrary, she came across as being positively changed for the better by it...like she was relieved that someone, at last, had so clearly seen right through her. It was as if her parched soul, dehydrated by the effects of a life besieged by bad relationships, had somehow been refreshed and revived with living water!

40. The Samaritans who believed then came to Him and asked Him to remain there with them, so He ended up staying there two days.

41. Then even more people in town began to believe that He was the Messiah because of the things that He said.

42. And they told the woman that they no longer believed just because of what she had initially told them, but because of the things that they heard Him say first hand during those two days. They declared to her that they were convinced that He was, indeed, the Savior of the world, the Christ, Himself, as she had suggested.

43. But after those days He went on from there into Galilee, which was His original plan and destination,

44. although He Himself acknowledged and declared that a prophet generally is dishonored in His own natural habitat.

45. But as it turned out when He got into Galilee, He actually found that the people sincerely welcomed Him there. It was apparent that their hearts had been completely opened up to Him, and they took His claims seriously because they had attended the feast in Jerusalem and had seen everything that He did there. The Jerusalem experience changed them, and they were ready to receive Jesus as the Christ.

46. So Jesus came again to Cana of Galilee where He had turned the water into wine. And there He encountered a certain royal official whose son was lying ill in Capernaum.

47. The man had heard that Jesus had returned from Judea and was again in Galilee, so he came to meet Him there and began to literally beg Jesus to come and heal his son because the boy was about to die.

48. Jesus said to him, "Unless you see signs and miracles, you people will never believe or have faith, at all."

49. The king's officer pleaded with Him, "Sir, I do have faith. That's why I have come to You to ask for Your help. You're my only hope at this point because if You don't come and heal him, my boy is going to die."

50. Jesus answered him, "All right. Go in peace. Your son will live!" And the man just took Jesus at His word, without seeing anything…no sign…no miracle. He simply put his trust in what Jesus had said and started home.

51. While he was still en route to his house, his servants met him on the way and said to him, "Your son is alive and well!"

52. When he inquired as to the exact time that his son had taken a turn for the better, they said to him, "The fever left him at one o'clock yesterday afternoon."

53. And the man immediately realized that that was exactly when Jesus had spoken the words, "Your son will live!" Needless to say, he and his whole household believed from that point on.

54. This was the second wonder that Jesus performed after He had come out of Judea into Galilee.

Chapter 5

1. A while later, Jesus traveled to Jerusalem for one of the Jewish festivals.

2. And there was in the city, near the Sheep Gate, a pool that is called Bethesda (in the Aramaic language).

3. This area was a well-known apparition site where a great number of sick people – the blind, the crippled, the paralyzed – did nothing every day but wait near the edge of the pool.

4. *(Verse #4 does not appear in the original manuscript.)* They waited there because of a widely believed myth about an angel that would periodically

and unexpectedly make the water in the pool bubble up, thereby giving it healing properties.

5. One who was there was a man who had been an invalid for thirty-eight years.

6. When Jesus saw him lying there at the pool and learned that he had been in that condition for so long, He asked him, "Would you like to be well and whole?"

7. The man said, "Sir, I have no one to help me into the pool when the water is stirred by the angel. As soon as I try to get in by myself, someone else always goes down ahead of me."

8. Jesus said to him, "Stop wasting your time by putting all your hope in this urban legend. You don't need to wait for some angel to make the water bubble up. Just stand up on your own two feet, take up your cot, and walk!"

9. As soon as Jesus spoke these words, the man was instantly healed. Now the day on which this took place was the Sabbath,

10. and, true to form, that technicality was all that the religious leaders noticed or cared about. They said to the man who had been healed, "It is the Sabbath and the law forbids that you carry your own cot."

11. But he replied, "The man who made me well said to me, 'Pick up your bed and walk,' and so I did!"

12. So they asked him, "Who told you to pick it up and walk?"

13. The man who was healed had absolutely no idea who it was, for Jesus had vanished into the crowd.

14. Later, Jesus found him at the temple and said to him, "Look at yourself! You are completely well! Now stop committing the sin of believing in myths and legends...of limiting your options by just focusing on one thing, like some magical, bubbling water, to help you. Repent, also, of the sin of believing that you are totally dependent on others to get you to where you

need to be in your life. This mindset of yours is more of a disability than anything that you've dealt with physically, and if you don't stop this sinful thinking, a worse thing will eventually come on you."

15. The man went away and told the Jewish leaders that it was Jesus who had caused him to be healed.

16. So, because Jesus was doing these things on the Sabbath, the religious leaders began to persecute Him.

17. Defending Himself to them, Jesus said, "My Father is always at work – every day, around the clock – and I am simply imitating His work patterns."

18. This is why they began to try to kill Him. He was not only trampling all over their limited concept of the Sabbath, He was just glibly calling God His own Father and, ultimately, making Himself equal with God.

19. Jesus answered them, "Look, here's the absolute truth about how I operate. The Son can do nothing by Himself; He can only do what He sees His Father doing. The Son just imitates the Father, that's all,

20. because the Father loves the Son and shows Him everything He does and how to do it. And He will even show Him greater works to perform in what you perceive to be the future – things that will totally amaze you.

21. "And just as the Father raises the dead, giving them life, so the Son creates life in whomever He pleases.

22. "Furthermore, the Father judges no one, but has entrusted all judgment to the Son, entirely.

23. "He has done this so that all people, everywhere, may honor the Son just as they honor the Father. Whoever does not honor the Son, does not honor the Father who sent Him.

24. "In all honesty I say to you, whoever hears My word, and believes in Him who sent Me, is walking in the fullness of eternal life and will never live out his or her life under a sentence of judgment.

25. "And, believe Me when I tell you this, the time is coming – in fact, the time is now – when those who have been dragging themselves through their days on earth like dead people because of the oppression of religion, will hear the Son's voice and will begin to really live for the first time in their lives.

26. "For as the Father has life in Himself, so He has granted the Son also to have life in Himself.

27. "And He has given Him authority to judge because He is the Son of Man – the One who empathizes with the human condition.

28. "Do not be amazed at this idea, for the time will come when all people – both the dead and the living – shall hear His voice

29. and shall ultimately be held accountable to Him for the way in which they live (or lived) out their lives.

30. "By Myself I am powerless; I judge only as I hear, and My judgment is fair and just because I have no selfish, hidden agenda. My entire motivation is to please Him who sent Me.

31. "If I testify only about Myself, My testimony is invalid and irrelevant.

32. "But there is another who testifies on My behalf and I know that His testimony about Me is all true.

33. "You have personally sent an inquiry to John, and he freely and publicly testified on My behalf.

34. "Not that I am dependent upon human testimony. I only mention it that you may have a point of reference for your own salvation.

35. "John was the lamp that burned…shining for all to see…illuminating the path to show you the way. And for a short time you were more than happy to bask in the warmth of that bright and unique light.

36. "But I have a mandate and a testimony that is weightier than that of John. For the very work that the Father has given Me to finish, which I am doing, confirms the fact that the Father has sent Me.

37. "And the One who sent Me – the Father Himself – has testified concerning Me. You have never heard or seen Him, no matter in what form He has appeared to you. You have never recognized any of His manifestations or revelations, so it stands to reason that you do not recognize His incarnation in Me.

38. "And you do not have His word living in your hearts because you do not acknowledge the Word that has become flesh, living and moving all around you.

39. "You religiously search the Scriptures because you believe that they produce life in you, but you do not recognize that the Scriptures are all about Me, the very source of life!

40. "You see Me and the works that I do, but you refuse to approach Me to find out how to really live your life.

41. "Look, I don't crave human validation. I don't have an overwhelming need to be famous or adored, or even accepted for that matter, because I already know who I am, whether you ever do or not. I do not need your approval.

42. "So I can tell you this without any fear of your rejection: I know you more than you can even understand. In fact, I know you better than you know yourselves, and I clearly see that there is no evidence of the love of God in you, whatsoever.

43. "I have come to you in My Father's name and you do not accept Me. But, interestingly, if someone else comes in his own name, speaking in no one's authority but his own, you don't seem to have any problem accepting him.

44. "But, really, it's not surprising. You all are so accustomed to living to please one another – to heaping glory and honor only on those who are in the loop, as it were, who are connected to the arc of your religious circle – that it never occurs to you that you should only be seeking the praise and glory of the

Father, God, alone.

45. "But I have no need or intention to accuse you to the Father. You already have an accuser, and his name is Moses, the one on whom you have built your entire religious system.

46. "The bottom line is this: If you believed Moses, you would believe Me, for he wrote about Me, personally.

47. "But if you do not really believe his writings, how can you ever believe My teachings?"

Chapter 6

1. After this, Jesus crossed to the other side of the Sea of Galilee, or Tiberias as it is also known,

2. and a great number of people began to follow Him because they were so amazed by the signs that they saw Him continually perform on the sick.

3. Then Jesus ascended to a mountainside and sat down with His disciples there.

4. It was near the time of the Passover Festival.

5. When Jesus noticed that a great crowd was coming toward Him, He said to Philip, "Listen, we have a situation; these people are hungry and we need to feed them right here, right now. Do you have any thoughts or suggestions about where we can buy bread for all of them to eat?"

6. He asked this only to test his faith and capacity for a big vision, for He already had a plan in His mind about what He was going to do.

7. Philip answered Him, "Do You realize that there are several thousand people here? I mean, we could feasibly do it, but it would take a great deal of planning and almost a year's wages to buy enough for each one to just have a bite!"

8. Another of His disciples, Andrew (Simon Peter's brother), spoke up and said,

9. "I don't know if this means anything or not, but You may want to know that there is a boy here with a lunch of five small barley loaves and two small fish. I know that this little bit of food certainly won't go very far among so many, but it's *something*. Just a thought...."

10. Jesus said, "All right then, have all the people sit down." It was a large, grassy area, and they all sat down there as they were instructed (if you counted just the men, there were about five thousand of them).

11. Then Jesus took the loaves, gave thanks, and began distributing bread to those who were seated. Thousands of them took as much as they wanted because there was no enforced rationing – literally, they had all they could eat! Then He took the fish and did exactly the same thing with it.

12. When everyone there had eaten all they could hold, He said to His disciples, "Now, gather up all the leftovers. Don't let anything go to waste."

13. So they gathered the scraps and excess food and filled up twelve whole baskets with thousands of pieces of bread and fish that were uneaten.

14. After the people saw this amazing sign, they began to say to one another, "You know, this man must surely be the Prophet whose coming the whole world has been expecting!"

15. Jesus, becoming aware of how profoundly affected the people were by this miracle, realized that they were going to try to apprehend Him and forcibly make Him their king. So He resisted the temptation to settle for any earthly kingship and withdrew again to a mountain by Himself. He needed to be alone to regain a little perspective on maintaining the balance between His humanity and His divinity.

16. When evening came, His disciples went down to the lake together,

17. where they boarded a boat and set off across the water

for Capernaum. It was now dark and Jesus had not yet joined them.

18. And a very strong wind started to blow hard across the water and began to produce extremely high, choppy whitecaps.

19. When they had rowed the boat out between three and three and a half miles, the disciples were astonished to see Jesus approaching the boat on foot! He was walking on top of the rough waves as if they were little hills on dry land! When they realized what He was doing, they just became totally paralyzed by overwhelming fear.

20. But He said to them, "Don't be afraid, boys! It's just Me!"

21. Then, as their initial panic began to subside, they were able to gather their wits enough to take Him into the boat. And in virtually no time, the vessel reached the shore where they were heading, landing in exactly the right spot.

22. The following day, the crowd that had stayed on the other side of the lake began to realize that only one boat had been there and that Jesus had not boarded it with His disciples. They remembered that the disciples had left without Him.

23. Then several boats from Tiberias arrived near the place where the people had eaten the miraculously-multiplied bread after the Lord had given thanks and blessed it.

24. As soon as the crowd realized that neither Jesus nor His disciples were there, they got into the boats and went to Capernaum, aggressively searching for Jesus.

25. When they finally found Him on the opposite side of the lake, they asked Him, "Teacher, when did You get here?"

26. Jesus answered, "Let Me tell you the truth: You are looking for Me, not because you saw the signs that I performed, but because you liked the fact that you ate

the bread and fish until you were full.

27. "You shouldn't strive so hard to find food that is only going to spoil in a couple of days; you should be using your energies to constantly search for the source of eternal food...the bread in the now...which the Son of Man will freely give you! And He gives you this bread because it is on Him that the Father has placed His unique seal of approval."

28. Then they asked Him, "How can we best use our energies to do the works that God requires of us?"

29. Jesus answered them, "The work of God, basically, is only this: to simply believe in the One whom He has sent."

30. So they said, "We assume that You are referring to Yourself, and if believing in You really is all that we should do to meet God's requirements, then what sign will You give to convince us of that? What supernatural wonder will You perform before our eyes that will leave us no choice but to believe in You?

31. "You see, our ancestors saw all manner of amazing signs in the wilderness, not the least of which was the manna that they ate daily, just as it is written: 'He gave them bread from heaven to eat.'"

32. Jesus said to them, "Surely, you must realize that it is not Moses who has given you the bread from heaven. Only My Father can give you the true, eternal bread in the now...the nourishment that comes from the heavenly realm...and He is serving you that real bread today.

33. "For the bread of God is He who has come from the eternal now, the One who has descended from the heavenly realm to give life to the whole world."

34. Jesus' words came across with such conviction and authority that the people who heard them enthusiastically responded by saying, "Then give us this heavenly bread now and forever!"

35. Jesus said to them, "You still don't get it! Don't you understand that this bread is not something that I can give you – it is what I am! I literally *am* the Bread of Life, and he or she who believes in Me will never go hungry or thirsty again…ever!

36. "But, as I have told you again and again, you have seen Me and My miracles, but somehow you can't seem to really believe that I am who I say that I am! You can't see beyond the limited boundaries of your preconceived, religious ideology!

37. "But everyone that the Father enlightens will come to Me, unrestricted by religion. And when they do come, no matter what and no matter from where, I will never, ever reject them in any way.

38. "For I have come down from the heavenly realm into this dimension not to do My will, but to do the will of Him who sent Me.

39. "And this is the will of Him who sent Me: that I should not lose anyone that He has given Me, but that I should give new life to them all, that I should raise them all up, even if bringing them all to salvation requires that I seek for them until there are no more days.

40. "For this is My Father's will – it is His ultimate purpose – that everyone who looks to the Son and believes in Him shall experience all the potential of eternal life, even if they don't see the fullness of it until the very last day."

41. Then suddenly He began to somehow lose favor with His audience. For the most part they had been somewhat open-minded to His message up until He said, "I, Myself, am the Bread that came down out of heaven!" For some reason, that particular statement seemed to rub everyone the wrong way, and the whole crowd began to turn on Him from that point.

42. They kept saying, "Isn't this Jesus, the Son of Joseph the carpenter? Doesn't He realize that we know both

of His parents and that we know where He came from? How can He have such delusions of grandeur; how can He be so out of touch with reality that He could say, 'I have come down from heaven'?"

43. So Jesus said to them, "Look, I know what you're thinking and I can hear the things that you are saying against Me to one another, and I want you to stop it right now!

44. "I'll say it again, whether you like it or not: No one is able to come to Me unless the Father who sent Me attracts them to Me, and I will eventually raise them all up, even if it requires a continual effort on My part, all the way up to the very last day!

45. "And this reconciliation is what the prophets of old referred to when they said, 'And they shall *all* be personally taught by God, Himself.'

46. "No one has seen the Father in His fullness except the One who is from God; only He has really seen the Father in all His glory.

47. "I am telling you the truth: He or she who believes in Me walks in the full blessings and benefits of everlasting life.

48. "And I reiterate, I *am* the Bread of Life!

49. "Look, I know that the manna in the wilderness is one of your most cherished and sacred iconic images, but you must face the fact that your forefathers ate it for years and died anyway!

50. "But I am talking about the bread that comes down out of heaven, which a person may eat and, as a result, will never die.

51. "Whether you are ready to receive it or not, it is a fact: I am the Living Bread that came out of the heavenly realm, or down from heaven, as you perceive it. If anyone eats this bread, he or she will live abundantly forever, and this bread literally is My *flesh* – the flesh that contains the life that I will lay down for the whole world."

52. Now the people became angry at Him because they were scandalized and appalled at this talk of "eating flesh." They considered the idea at once bizarre and grotesque and said to one another, "How is He able to give us His flesh to eat?"

53. And Jesus said to them, "This is the truth, regardless of how strange it may sound to your ears: You cannot have any life in you unless you devour the flesh of the Son of Man. And not only that, but you must also drink His blood if you want to live!

54. "The person who is hungry enough to feed on My flesh and thirsty enough to drink My blood, will walk in the full potential of eternal life and I will ultimately and personally raise him or her up.

55. "For My flesh is real, genuine food, and My blood is real, genuine drink.

56. "He or she who feeds on My flesh and drinks My blood dwells continually in Me and I will dwell continually in him or her.

57. "Just as My living Father sent Me and I live because of Him, so the one who feeds on Me will live because of Me. I am the sustainer of life!

58. "You're literally looking at the bread that came down out of heaven. And this bread is not like the manna which your and My ancestors ate and still died. The individual who relies on this bread for his or her primary food source will live now and forever."

59. He said all this while He was teaching in the synagogue in Capernaum.

60. When His disciples heard this, many of them said, "He's just gone too far this time with this strange doctrine. His self-exaltation alone is blasphemous enough to be deemed inappropriate and unacceptable for most people, but this allusion to cannibalism and vampirism is, frankly, just too hard for anyone to stomach!"

61. Aware that His disciples were having this

conversation, He confronted them, asking, "Do we have a problem? Is My teaching offensive to you?

62. "I mean, if My revelation is too radical for you to receive, then how are you going to deal with it when you see the Son of Man literally ascend to where He was before?

63. "My teaching is transcendent and spiritual, and it is the Spirit that gives life. Speaking about the trivialities of dead religion and the superficiality of the flesh does not profit you in any way. It is a waste of time. The words that I speak, however, are literally filled with the Spirit and they are full of the essence of life!

64. "And yet, in spite of the accessibility to the spirit-world that My words provide, there are still some of you, amazingly, who do not believe."

65. He went on to say, "This is why I have told you that no one can come to Me unless they can embrace the broader scope – the bigger picture if you will – where the Father can attract them to Me."

66. At this time many of His disciples disassociated themselves from Him and had nothing more to do with Him.

67. But Jesus made no effort to explain Himself or to qualify His offensive statements to the remaining disciples. And, without any apology, retraction or attempt at clarification, He asked the twelve, flatly, "Well? Are you leaving with the rest of them?"

68. Peter spoke up and said, "Are You joking? Where would we go? There's nothing else to look for after finding You because You alone have the words of life for us; for us, You are the journey's end.

69. "We don't have to understand everything that You say with our minds because we believe in You with our hearts. Regardless of anything You throw at us, and no matter how new or strange it may sound to our ears, we have come to know, without a doubt, that

You are the Christ...the Anointed One...the Son of the living God."

70. Then Jesus said, "Well, you twelve are the original ones that I personally chose in the beginning. You are special to Me because you are the ones I started out with, even though I know that one of you is My adversary."

71. He was referring to Judas (the son of Simon Iscariot), who eventually betrayed Him, even though he was one of the originals.

Chapter 7

1. After this, Jesus went around in Galilee, intentionally avoiding Judea because the locals there were wanting to kill Him.

2. But when the Jewish Feast of Tabernacles was near,

3. Jesus' brothers took Him aside and said to Him, "You know, this really is no place for You. The masses are never going to see You here. You really ought to leave this small town and go to Judea, so that more of Your followers there can see the miracles that You perform.

4. "No one who wants the publicity that it takes to become a public figure does anything low profile or in secret. If You feel you must do these things...if You're determined to keep acting like this...then go all the way with it! Make it work for You and reveal Yourself to the world!"

5. They had this little talk with Him, basically, because they did not believe in Him or take Him seriously. His very own brothers couldn't recognize His divinity or His uniqueness.

6. So, He replied to them, "My time has not come, yet. But because you, My brothers, do not understand the delicacy of timing or the importance of seasons...and

really because You do not understand who I really am…any time is suitable for you. You think that the window of opportunity is always open.

7. "You don't have any idea what it is like to be hated by the world. You blend in so well with the status quo that society has no reason to form any opinion, positive or negative, about you. But the larger society, especially the part that has been shaped by the conformity of religion, definitely hates Me. It hates Me, not just because of My individuality, but because I expose it for what it is, with all of its hypocrisy and phoniness.

8. "Please feel free to go to the feast yourselves. There will be a lot of people there who think just like you do, so you should be able to enjoy yourselves. But I have no intention of going because it is premature for Me to go public, and there is no way that I can go there privately or without being noticed. You couldn't possibly understand this because you don't lead public lives, but I have to strategically plan My every move so that I can stay in My proper time."

9. Having said this to them, He stayed behind in Galilee.

10. But afterward, when His brothers had gone up to the feast without Him, He actually did go there, also. Without traveling in their caravan, and without being a part of any entourage, it was more possible for Him to maintain anonymity and not draw attention to Himself.

11. But, of course, He was the One that everyone was already talking about…the One that everyone had come there to see. They kept asking, "Where is that man, that radical, that miracle-worker? Is He here? Is He coming?"

12. And there was an amazing amount of buzz about Him everywhere at the celebration. Little groups were huddled all over the place, arguing about Him in hushed tones so that the Jewish religious leaders

could not hear, but in hot dispute over Him, nonetheless. Some said, "He is good!" Others said, "No, He is a deceiver who spreads false ideas!"

13. But no one had the courage to make any public statement about Him one way or the other.

14. But when the feast was about half over, to everyone's surprise, Jesus went up into the temple court and just began to teach.

15. The Jews there were astonished at His presentation. They said, "How is it that this unlearned man can sound so intelligent and inspired? How can He be so eloquent when speaking of the sacred and the spiritual, especially when He expounds on theology and the Holy Scriptures?"

16. Jesus overheard them and said, "I can't take any credit for My teaching, because it is not My own but is the teaching of Him who sent Me.

17. "If anyone desires to please God by doing His will, he or she will be illuminated to recognize whether or not My teaching is from God. Those who desire to hear from God will have the insight and discernment to properly judge My doctrine and to be able to identify its supernatural source.

18. "He who speaks on his own authority does so with a hidden agenda, to gain honor for himself. But he who speaks for the honor of the one who sent him is a man of truth and integrity. There is nothing false – nothing to be mistrusted – about him.

19. "And while I'm on the subject of integrity, let Me ask those of you who want to kill Me a question. We all agree that Moses gave you the law, but you all know good and well that not one of you keeps it, so why do you think that you should kill Me because you presume that I don't keep the law? What is the source of this hypocritical and irrational anger towards Me?"

20. Immediately the attitude of the crowd went negative, and they answered Him, "You are a paranoid lunatic!

Who wants to kill You? You must be demon-possessed!"

21. Jesus answered them, "Look, I did one miracle and you were all astounded by it.

22. "Now Moses established the rite of circumcision, although he did not originate it (the Patriarchs did), and you are totally fine with performing it on baby boys on the Sabbath.

23. "So explain to Me how you can circumcise one part of a child's body on the Sabbath so that Moses' law will not be broken, and yet be so angry at Me because I healed a man's whole body on the Sabbath?

24. "I mean, think about it! If you can stop judging everything by the superficial appearance of religion for one minute, you can see how absurd and pointless religion can be. Only then can you judge Me fairly."

25. Just then, ironically, some other people from Jerusalem joined the crowd and inadvertently confirmed His initial accusation by saying, "Hey, isn't that the man that they're trying to kill?

26. "And here He is speaking right out here in the open…in the temple…right in front of the religious leaders! Did we miss something? Have the authorities now concluded that He is the Messiah?

27. "But the fact *is* that we know where this man is originally from, and we know that when the Messiah comes, no one should be able to know where He comes from!"

28. Then Jesus, still in the middle of His teaching in the temple courts, cried out to them, "You think you know Me because you think you know where I am from. What you don't know is that I am not here on My own authority, but He who sent Me is true – the consummation of all the truth – and because you don't know His truth, you don't know Me or understand where I am really from!

29. "But that does not affect My self-awareness because I do know Him, and I know without a doubt that He sent Me here."

30. These words were like a cue to the crowd to become aggressively violent with Him. They actually tried to personally seize Him with their own hands, but no one could get a grip on Him because His time had not come yet.

31. But somehow, in spite of all this, there actually were many in the crowd who began to believe in Him that day. They made this point, saying, "When the Messiah does come, does anyone really think that He could perform more extravagant and impressive signs and wonders than this man does and has?"

32. By this time the Pharisees had become aware of what the people in the temple courts were saying about Him, both pro and con, so they decided to put a stop to all of it. The chief priests, along with the Pharisees, sent the temple guards to arrest Him on the spot so that He would no longer be the controversial center of attention at this traditional celebration.

33. But Jesus made this final statement for that day: "I am only with you here in this dimension for a short time, and then I am going back to be reunited with the One who sent Me.

34. "You will look for Me then, but you will not be able to find Me because where I am going, you cannot come."

35. Upon hearing this dramatic statement, the people there said, "Where does this man think He can go that we can't find Him? Will He go to where the Jews live scattered among the Greeks so that He can teach the Greeks?

36. "And what does He mean by saying, 'You will look for Me, but you will not find Me'? And why did He say, 'Where I am, you cannot come'?" And they argued and speculated and tried to interpret His words

for the rest of that day. But He was nowhere to be found.

37. But on the final and most important day of the feast, Jesus just stood up right where He was and, without any timidity or self-consciousness at all, began to yell out at the top of His lungs these words: "Let anyone who is thirsty come to Me and drink!

38. "Whoever believes in Me, as the Scriptures have stated, living rivers of life will continuously and freely flow from within their inner beings!"

39. This was His way of introducing them to the ministry of the Holy Spirit, who, those who believed in Him would later receive. The era of the Holy Spirit had not yet begun at this time, since Jesus had not yet been glorified.

40. On hearing these startling words spoken so loudly, some of the people said, "Surely this man is the Prophet!"

41. Others said, "No, He is the Messiah!" Still others argued, "But, how can the Messiah come from Galilee?

42. "Doesn't the Scripture say that the Messiah will come from the descendants of David…from Bethlehem, the town where David lived?"

43. So the people, forced into forming an opinion about Jesus with their limited understanding of how His life had already confirmed the Scriptures, were ultimately divided because of Him.

44. Some wanted to seize or arrest Him, but no one had the courage to lay a hand on Him.

45. Finally, the temple guards went back to the Pharisees and chief priests, who asked them, "Well, where is He? Why didn't you bring Him in?"

46. "It's hard to explain," the guards replied. "If you could only hear Him for yourselves – if you could see the way that the people relate and respond to Him…even the way that He invokes all kinds of

reactions from them – you would understand that there has just never been a person, anywhere or anytime, who speaks like this man!"

47. "Don't tell me that He has deceived you, also!" retorted one of the Pharisees.

48. "You certainly don't see any of us believing in Him, do you?

49. "It's only this stupid crowd – gullible people who are ignorant of our precious law – that even considers His ridiculous claims. And may they be damned for it!"

50. Nicodemus, who had gone to Jesus earlier and was one of the Pharisees, said,

51. "Surely our law does not condemn a man without giving him a fair trial first! Shouldn't we at least hear Him ourselves to find out what He is actually doing?"

52. They replied, "Nicodemus, we don't care how open-minded you may be about the prospect of a Prophet or Messiah coming out of Galilee; the fact remains that, if you look into it from a theological or historical viewpoint, you will clearly see that it is impossible for such a man to come from there!"

53. That being said, the meeting broke up and they all went home.

The earliest manuscripts and many other ancient witnesses do not contain John 7:53-8:11

Chapter 8

1. Instead of returning to His home after the feast as everyone else did, Jesus went to the Mount of Olives.

2. But first thing the next morning, He was right back again in the temple courts drawing a crowd to Himself. And when the people who were there at that hour began to gather around Him, He sat down to teach them.

3. While He was in the middle of His talk, a group of some of the scribes and Pharisees dramatically interrupted His message by bringing a woman up to Him that they had somehow managed to catch in the act of adultery. They made her stand before Him in the middle of the court as if she were on trial in front of a judge.

4. And, with obvious sarcasm, they called Him, "Teacher," and said, "this woman has been caught in the very act of adultery" (of course, no one made any mention of the *man* with whom she was caught "in the act").

5. But they continued, "In our law, Moses commanded us to stone such adulterous women to death. But we have brought this woman to You because we want to know what *You* have to say about her fate."

6. They were using this question to trap Him, intellectually and theologically, in front of an audience. But Jesus, instead of getting into a heated debate with them, just stooped down and began to write rather mysteriously on the ground with His finger, as if the religious men weren't even there.

7. But His ignoring them in this manner only caused them to become more persistent in their questioning. So He stood back up, looked around at all of them, and said, "Yes. I would say that it is both appropriate and necessary to stone her with stones until she is dead, as Moses commanded. And I also think that since you are the ones who discovered her in her indiscretion, then you are the ones most qualified to perform the execution…so step right up and start the killing! And whichever one of you is absolutely sinless should have the honor of hurling the first stone at her."

8. Then He bent down again and went on writing on the ground with His finger.

9. His words just seemed to hang, suspended in the air,

and the power of them deflated the pompous arrogance of the men who had apprehended the woman. Conviction gripped their hearts and, while Jesus paid no attention to them as He continued His writing, they just began to silently file out of the temple court, one by one, from the oldest down to the last one.

10. When Jesus stood back up, He looked straight at the woman and said to her, "Ma'am where are your accusers? Has no man in this crowd pronounced a sentence of condemnation on you?"

11. She looked around and then answered Him, "Apparently no one, Sir." "Then I don't condemn you, either," He replied. "You see, condemnation for the sin of adultery, or any other sin for that matter, doesn't come from above – from My Father or from Me – it comes from the people around you. People remit sins and people retain sins, depending on how they feel about you and on how they interpret their religion. My advice to you is that you change your adulterous lifestyle, because it's only going to bring you pain, and people can be very unforgiving of your mistakes. Now go, and don't get yourself into this kind of trouble again."

12. Then He turned His attention back to the crowd who was still there listening and said, "I am the Light of the world. Whoever follows Me will never stumble around in darkness, blinded by the hypocrisy and self-righteousness of religious thinking, but will have the light of life."

13. But there were other Pharisees there in the crowd who defied Him by saying, "You are testifying on Your own behalf, so Your testimony is invalid. We can't just be expected to take Your word for it that You are who You claim to be."

14. Jesus answered, "My testimony is true, even if I do testify on My own behalf. And I can speak up for

Myself with authority because I know where I came from and I know where I am going. You just can't receive it because you don't know where I came from and so you don't know where I am going. You have no real comprehension of Me because of your lack of perception.

15. "You evaluate everything by human standards, setting yourselves up to judge according to the flesh. You have no point of reference other than what you can see with the natural eye. But I do not set Myself up to judge anyone or to pass a sentence of condemnation on them.

16. "But even if I take the liberty to sit in judgment, My judgment will be true and undisputed and I will always make the right decision. I say that with all confidence because I am not alone in the decision-making process...there are two of us. The Father who sent Me is in complete harmony with Me. We confer on everything and we agree on everything.

17. "And in your own law it is written that the corroborating testimony of two witnesses is reliable enough to stand up in court.

18. "I am one of the two necessary parties bearing testimony concerning Myself. The other validating witness is My Father who sent Me, and He is consistent with His testimony in My behalf."

19. Then they said to Him, "You keep talking about this Father of Yours...well, where is He?" Jesus answered them, "You have no perception of My Father because you have a misguided perception of Me. If you could see and know Me, you could see and know My Father. It's that simple."

20. This session took place in the Treasury, the place where the offerings were put in the temple court. But even though His teaching was not received there, no one ventured to arrest Him because His hour had not yet come.

21. Then once again He said to them, "I am leaving this dimension and returning to the heavenly realm, and you will look for Me, but you will die in the sin of your rebellion. With your state of mind, you cannot go where I am going."

22. At these words, the religious leaders began to ask among themselves, "Is He trying to tell us that He plans to commit suicide? Is that why He says that we cannot go where He is going?"

23. But He said to them, "You are from below...from the natural realm...bound by space and time...bound in your thinking by religion and the limitations of the law. I am from above...from the superior spirit-realm...the eternal now...the ultimate dimension. You are the prisoner of this world order. I am not of this world.

24. "That is why I have told you that you will die, having lived your entire life under the curse of your sins. If you do not believe that I am who I claim to be, that will be your fate."

25. So they said to Him, "Who are You, anyway? What are You really all about?" Jesus replied, "You know, speaking to you is just a waste of My time. I am exactly who and what I have been telling you over and over again. Why do you need for Me to keep repeating Myself?

26. "I could say a lot about you – words of harsh judgment that would all be true – but He who sent Me is faithful and trustworthy and so I choose to use My energies in telling the world the beautiful things that I have heard from Him, instead of spinning My wheels trying to convince you of something that you refuse to believe."

27. But even after all of this exchange, they still did not perceive that He was speaking to them of the Father.

28. So Jesus added, "When you have finally lifted up the Son of Man (He was speaking of being lifted up on

the cross), then you will know that I am who I have said all along that I am. I have no reason to lie to you, nothing to gain by misleading you. Eventually, you will understand that I do nothing that is self-motivated or on My own authority. I only say what My Father has taught Me. I have no other agenda.

29. "And He who has sent Me is always with Me. I'm not out here on My own, because I always only do what pleases Him."

30. While all of this conflict was going on between Jesus and the religious leaders, there were many in the crowd who, amazingly, began to believe in Him that day. Somehow, in spite of the negative atmosphere and extreme tension in the air, the truth of His message got through to them.

31. So He said to those who opened their hearts to Him then and there, "If you simply believe My words and wholeheartedly embrace My ideas, you will truly be My disciples.

32. "Then you will be freed from the bondage of religious thinking. Your knowledge of Me will become your key of truth...the key that opens the door to your mental and spiritual prison. In other words, you shall know the truth and the truth that you know will set you free!"

33. But others in the crowd answered Him, "We are the descendants of Abraham and have never been in bondage to anyone or to any ideology. What do You mean by saying that we will be 'set free'?"

34. Jesus replied, "Everyone who sees the world through the paradigm of the law and its consequences, eats from the tree of the knowledge of good and evil. So, when he or she sins, that person automatically becomes the slave of sin.

35. "And a slave has no permanent place in the family, but a son is a son indefinitely, no matter what he does. I have come to deliver you from the bondage of

slavery and to bring you into the Father's own family.

36. "You have a certain concept of freedom in your collective consciousness, but the Son is offering you a whole other and greater dimension of freedom. And if the Son liberates you, you will be liberated indeed…completely! You will no longer eat from the tree of the knowledge of good and evil, but you will eat from the tree of life! No longer slaves, you will know freedom in a way that you know nothing about at this point.

37. "I appreciate the fact that you are Abraham's descendants, but some of you would rather kill Me than to open your hearts to the freshness of My word! Don't you see how warped religious thinking can be?

38. "I tell you things that I have seen and heard, first hand, from being in the presence of My Father. Your actions reflect that you are just repeating what you have heard from *your* father."

39. Indignant, they retorted, "Abraham is our father!" But Jesus replied, "If you really were the children of Abraham, then you would live like Abraham lived…you would do what he did. Abraham was open to change and had a real relationship with God. He actually conversed with the Father and could receive revelation from Him. He didn't just mindlessly follow a form of rules and regulations.

40. "But now there are some of you who are looking for an efficient way to kill Me…One who has told you things that I heard fresh from God, Himself! Abraham would have had an open mind and would have listened to Me.

41. "You are actually acting like your real father." They said to Him, "Are You calling us bastards? You should know that we have no Father but God!"

42. Jesus said to them, "No, if God were your Father, you would love Me and receive Me as your own brother. I came from God, straight from His very presence. I

am not self-appointed. The One that you say is your Father is the One who sent Me!

43. "Why are My words so confusing to you? Why do they make you so angry? It's because your rigid, religious mindset will not allow you to hear Me with your heart!

44. "You are the offspring of your father, that devil called religion! You carry out the devil's desires, which have always culminated in murder – from Cain's murdering Abel over the proper way to offer the sacrifice, to your current plans to assassinate Me! That murdering devil is the father of lies; lying is his natural inclination, and when he lies, he speaks in his native tongue!

45. "So when I tell you the *truth,* you don't believe Me. You are so saturated with lies that the truth sounds false to your religious ears.

46. "Not one of you can prove Me guilty of sin, so why don't you believe Me when I tell you the truth?

47. "Whoever belongs to God hears the voice of God. You can't recognize My voice because you do not really belong to God."

48. They answered Him, "Do You know what we think? We think that You are a Samaritan and that You are demon-possessed!"

49. Jesus said, "Well, I'm definitely not a Samaritan and, no, I am not possessed by a demon. All I am is one who honors My Father and, for that, you dishonor Me.

50. "I have no desire to seek glory for Myself. There is only One who does that and He, alone, is the Judge.

51. "And the truth is that whoever receives and obeys My word will never see death."

52. At this they exclaimed, "Well, You may not be a Samaritan, but You definitely are demon-possessed! Now we know that You are because of what You just said. Abraham died and so did all the prophets, yet

You say that whoever obeys Your word will never die!

53. "Are You claiming to be greater than our father Abraham? Hello…he died! The prophets died! Who do You think You are to say such an outrageous thing?"

54. Jesus replied, "Look, here's the bottom line: If I glorify Myself, My glory is empty and meaningless. But My Father, whom you claim is your God, is the One who glorifies Me, and that's all the validation that I need.

55. "You do not know Him, but I do. I can't say that I don't because then I would be lying like you. It's the truth, whether you believe it or not. I know that I know Him and that I obey His word.

56. "Furthermore, your father Abraham rejoiced at the thought of seeing My day and hour, and he did actually see it and it was everything that he hoped it would be."

57. The Jewish leaders then shouted out, "You are not even fifty years old! How could You have personally seen Abraham who lived centuries ago...and how could he possibly have seen You or Your 'day'? You're unbelievable!"

58. "I'm just telling you the truth," Jesus calmly replied. "And the truth is that, before Abraham was even born, I AM!"

59. Well, that statement just pushed them over the edge. They not only considered it an insanely arrogant thing to say, but it struck them as being blatantly blasphemous to use the holy words "I AM" when referring to Himself. They became so infuriated that they started picking up stones to stone Him with, but Jesus, once again, was miraculously able to slip away from the midst of the people on the temple grounds.

Chapter 9

1. As He was walking along one day, Jesus saw a man who had been blind since birth.

2. His disciples, picking up on the object of His attention, asked Him, "Teacher, whose sin caused this man's blindness? Was his own sinfulness the source of the problem, or did he inherit some generational curse from his sinful parents?"

3. Jesus answered them, "Why do you assume that his blindness is the direct result of sin? And even if it *were* the result of sin, why is it so important to you to know *whose* sin it was? You need to change your perspective and your priorities. When you see someone in need like this, your immediate response should be to look for a way for the works of God to be displayed in his or her life, and nothing more.

4. "As long as it is daylight, we must do the work of Him who sent Me, and His work is to heal the whole of humanity, not to punish people who are already suffering. God's business is the order of the day and it must be done before nightfall.

5. "And as long as I am in this dimension, I am the world's light."

6. When He had said this, He did something quite unusual; He spat on the ground and made mud with His saliva, then He spread it all over the man's eyes.

7. After that, He sent the man to wash in the pool of Siloam (which, ironically, means "Sent"). So he went and did as Jesus had instructed him and he came back with fully restored vision.

8. When the neighbors and people who only knew him by sight as a blind beggar saw him, they said, "Hey, isn't that the man who used to sit and beg so pathetically?"

9. Some said, "Yes! I think it *is* him!" Others said, "No

way! It has to be someone who just looks very much like that guy." But he, himself, settled the question by telling everyone, "Yes, I am the man who used to be blind!"

10. So they said to him, "What happened? How did you get your sight restored to you?"

11. He replied, "You know that man called Jesus? Well, He just made some mud and put it on my eyes and told me to go to Siloam and wash, which I did. And when I opened my eyes after flushing them out with water, I could see everything!"

12. Obviously excited, they asked, "Where is Jesus right now?" And he said to them, "How should I know?"

13. So they just sort of overtook the man who had been blind and brought him immediately to the Pharisees.

14. Now it just so happened that it was on the Sabbath day that Jesus mixed the mud and healed the man's eyes with it.

15. So the Pharisees asked the man what everyone else had asked him. They wanted to hear from him how he had received his sight, so he recounted to them the whole story of the mud and the miracle.

16. Then some of the Pharisees said, "Well, this Jesus that everyone keeps talking about is obviously not from God because He has no apparent regard for the Sabbath." But others said, "Yes, but how could a sinner or an evil man do such wonderful signs and miracles? How could a bad man do such good things?" So, there was, again, the typical difference of opinion and division over Jesus among them.

17. So they asked the man who had been healed, "What do you have to say about Him, seeing that it was your eyes that He opened?" And he said to them, "Well, there's clearly something special about Him...He must be a prophet!"

18. But the Jewish religious leaders did not believe that he had really been blind and was now healed. So they

called in his parents to verify the story.

19. When the parents arrived, the Pharisees said to them, "We have three questions for you: One, is this your son? Two, if he is your son, is it true that he was blind from birth? And three, if he was blind, how do you explain the fact that he can now see?"

20. The man's parents replied, "We can only answer the first two questions. He is definitely our son, and he has been completely blind from the day he was born.

21. "But, as for your third question, we have absolutely no idea what to tell you. We don't know how he is suddenly able to see after all these years, and we do not know who is responsible for this miracle. He is of age; you'll have to ask him about what has happened to him."

22. They said this in an effort to avoid acknowledging Jesus to the Pharisees. They were afraid of a confrontation, because the religious leaders had already agreed that if anyone should even hint that Jesus was the Christ, they would be banned from the synagogue.

23. So they dodged answering the question by saying, "He is of age; ask him."

24. So the Pharisees summoned the man a second time and said to him, "In the future, when people ask you about your restored eyesight, you must simply say that it was the result of a mysterious act of God. Do not give any credit to this Jesus, because He is sinful and wicked and should not receive any credit or publicity."

25. The man replied, "Look, I don't know if He is a sinner or not. And I'm not personally qualified to determine whether He is good or bad. All I can tell you is that this time last week I couldn't see a thing, and this week I have perfect eyesight! I have no opinion about His morality, character or ethics, and I don't know what He thinks about the Sabbath. But

one thing I can definitely vouch for is His ability to demonstrate the miraculous, even if His methods are unconventional! I mean, the man can heal people; in fact, He probably can do anything!"

26. So they said to him, "All right, off the record, tell us exactly what happened to you. Walk us through the entire encounter with Jesus from the beginning."

27. He answered, "Gentlemen, I've already told you this whole story! Why do you want me to repeat it? It sounds to me like you are interested only in Jesus, because you seem to be nearly obsessed with Him! If I didn't know better, I'd say that you are all considering becoming His disciples yourselves!"

28. Well, that did it! The Pharisees completely lost control at these words and cursed the man, railing at him with unbridled rage. "How dare you?" they snarled. "You're the one who is obsessed with Him! We are the disciples of Moses,

29. because we know that Moses was directly sent by God. We don't have any idea where this imposter, this Jesus, is from or what His wicked agenda is!"

30. The man replied, "You people are just too much! I mean, isn't this an amazing thing? Here this man has opened my eyes – you can't deny that – but you deny that you know where He came from! Amazing!

31. "Get serious! You have to know, deep down, that this man is the Christ! You don't believe that God listens to sinners, so how can you explain God listening to Him?

32. "Since the beginning of time, no one has ever opened the eyes of a man born blind. You know that it's true.

33. "If this man were not from God, there is no way that He could perform such miracles...pure and simple! There is nothing else that needs to be said about it."

34. They retorted, "You weren't just born blind...you were born in sin and you're still a sinner. How dare you presume to teach us! Who do you think you are?

This conversation is over!" And with that, they literally threw him out of the temple.

35. When Jesus heard that the man had been put out so dramatically, He went to meet him. When He found him, He asked, "Do you believe that the Son of Man is the Son of God?"

36. The man replied, "If He is who I think that He is, then point Him out to me and I will believe in Him."

37. Jesus said to him, "I believe you know who He is... He is talking to you right now!"

38. The man then cried out, "Lord, I do believe! And I worship You! You have not only given me my sight, You have given me back my life! You are the Christ, the Son of the Living God!"

39. Jesus responded, "I came to heal the blindness of the whole world and, in so doing, I have become a divider. I divide the light from the darkness so that those who have never seen can have their spiritual eyes opened and those who are supposedly the 'seers' will be exposed as the blind guides that they are."

40. Some nosy Pharisees were standing close by, eavesdropping on this conversation. They spoke up and said, "Are we to assume, then, that You are calling all of us blind?"

41. Jesus said, "No, actually, because if you all really were blind, you would be held blameless in your rejection of Me. But since you claim to have insight from God – because you are supposed to be the ones who can see the truth – you are held accountable. You are not blind...you just refuse to see."

Chapter 10

1. "Listen, all of you Pharisees, because I want to talk to you about so-called spiritual leaders who are really nothing more than thieves and robbers, and what I tell

you about them is the absolute truth. Simply put, anyone who does not enter in by the door into the sheepfold, but climbs up some other way, exposes himself as being nothing but a thief and a robber.

2. "But he or she who enters by the door is a true shepherd of sheep.

3. "The gatekeeper will open the gate for that shepherd, and his sheep will listen for the sound of his voice. And that true shepherd will call his own sheep by name, and he will lead them from the safety and security of the sheepfold, out into the wide, open spaces where green pastures can be found.

4. "And once he has brought his sheep outside, he will walk on ahead of them on the journey and they will automatically follow him because they recognize his voice and have learned to depend on his leadership to guide them.

5. "There is no chance of them ever following a stranger, because they would not recognize his voice and would be unfamiliar with his call. In fact, they would run away from him."

6. Jesus used this parable to illustrate the relationship between leaders with insight and integrity and their faithful followers, but it went right over the Pharisees' heads.

7. So Jesus broke it down for them and said, "The truth is that I, Myself, am the Door for the sheep.

8. "Anyone who ever came before or after Me claiming to be the door, was and is nothing but a dishonest thief and an opportunistic robber. But those sheep who are really hungry for spiritual food will not even listen to them.

9. "I am the Door. Anyone who enters in directly through Me, instead of trying to come in through his or her dogma, doctrine or denomination, will be saved. And that person will have the liberty to go in and out of different, progressive stages of truth to find

pasture.

10. "But these 'thieves and robbers,' as I call them, who impose the agendas of their own particular religious ideas and their irrelevant, man-made laws on the sheep, only do so in order to steal, kill and destroy them. They come to steal any and all prophetic revelation available to the sheep, to kill any chance of them ever having a real, first-hand relationship with God, and to ultimately destroy their personal destinies. But I have come that the sheep, the true seekers, may have and enjoy life and have it in abundance! Overflowing life…rich and full and free of religious oppression…that's the kind of life I have to offer the sheep who follow Me.

11. "I am the Good Shepherd. The good shepherd doesn't just lead the sheep, he actually risks and even lays down his own life for them.

12. "But when a servant who is only a hired hand sees a wolf coming, he deserts the flock and runs away, because he has no real relationship with the sheep. Then that wolf is able to catch the sheep and scatter them, and when they get separated from one another, they become particularly vulnerable.

13. "The hired hand flees because it's just a job to him. He doesn't have the connection with the sheep, nor the concern for them that a true shepherd does, because he does not own them and has no history with them.

14. "But I am the Good Shepherd, and I know and recognize My own sheep, and My own sheep know and recognize Me,

15. in the very same way that the Father knows Me and I know the Father. That is why I am able to give up My very life for the sheep.

16. "And not only that, but I also have other sheep besides these of whom I speak…sheep that you don't even know or believe exist because they are not of

this fold. But I must bring them in, also, and they will listen to My voice and will respond to the call that is uniquely meant for them. And they will be brought in to unite with these so that, ultimately, there will just be one great flock under one good shepherd.

17. "The Father loves Me because I lay down My life for My own, only to take it back up again for them.

18. "But make no mistake about this: No one takes My life from Me! I am the only one authorized to lay it down, and I do so voluntarily. I, alone, have the power to give up My life, and I willingly offer it as a sacrifice. I will never be a martyr. And because I have the power to lay it down, I have the power to take it back up again. I have received this command to take authority over My own death and resurrection from My Father."

19. Once again his audience was divided over His bold declarations.

20. Many of them held to the rumors that He was demon-possessed. Others said, "Why are you still listening to Him? Don't you realize that He is just a raving lunatic?"

21. But still others said, "It's ridiculous and entirely too easy to dismiss this man as being nothing more than a madman. And if you really think about it, the 'demon-possessed' theory can't fly either, because a demon could never open the eyes of the blind!"

22. Then came the Festival of Dedication of the reconstruction of the temple in Jerusalem.

23. It was winter, and Jesus was walking in the temple area called Solomon's Porch.

24. So the people who were there surrounded Him and began asking, "How long are You going to keep us in suspense? If You really are the Christ...the Messiah ...then open up to us and tell us plainly."

25. Jesus answered them, "You're not in suspense! I've repeatedly told you who I am; you just don't believe

Me. And I don't even need to tell you with words in the first place because My actions speak much louder to this issue. The works that I do in the name of the Father testify of Me.

26. "But you do not believe because you are not My sheep.

27. "My sheep intimately know My voice; I know them completely, and they willingly follow Me.

28. "I cause them to walk in the full potential of eternal life, and they will never be stolen from Me, or killed, or destroyed…because no one, not even you thieves and robbers, can snatch them out of My hand!

29. "My Father, who has given them to Me, is greater than anyone or any religious system; and no one can snatch them out of My Father's hand.

30. "The Father and I are one."

31. Once again, the people started picking up stones with which to stone Him when He said that.

32. But Jesus said to them, "I have shown you many amazing things and have done many good deeds in your presence because the Father has enabled Me to do so. For which miracle or act of mercy do you intend to stone Me?"

33. They answered, "We are not stoning You for any good work, but for Your blasphemy! You are a mere man, but You claim to be God!"

34. Jesus said to them, "Why do My claims shock and anger you so much? This isn't a new concept. Don't you know that in your own law – in the Psalms of Asaph – that God is recorded as saying, 'I said you were gods'?

35. "Now, if He called those who just received His message 'gods' in the Scriptures – in your own law – and you say that you honor the Scriptures and that the law cannot be set aside,

36. then how is it when I say that I am the Son of God whom the Father has set apart and sent into this

dimension, that you accuse Me of blasphemy?

37. "Look, don't believe Me unless I do the works of My Father.

38. "But if I do them, they alone should convince you that the Father is in Me and I am in the Father."

39. Once again, their anger was ignited and they tried to seize Him and, once again, He was able to escape their grasp.

40. After that, Jesus went back to the other side of the Jordan to the place where John had been baptizing earlier, and stayed in that location.

41. And many people came to Him there and said, "Although John never performed a sign, everything that he said about this man is true."

42. And in that place many people became believers in Him.

Chapter 11

1. Now Jesus had a personal friend named Lazarus, who was very sick. Lazarus lived in Bethany, the village of Mary and her sister, Martha.

2. This Mary was the one who, in this account of Jesus' life, anointed Him with perfume and wiped His feet with her hair. It was Mary's brother, Lazarus, who was sick, and Jesus was close to the whole family.

3. So when Lazarus became ill, his sisters sent word to Jesus, saying, "Lord, the friend whom You love so deeply is sick and needs Your help."

4. When Jesus received the message, He responded, prophetically, "This sickness will not end in death! In fact, it is for God's glory so that God's Son may be glorified through it."

5. Now it should be reiterated that Jesus loved these three people very much. He was close to them in a way that was rather unusual and unprecedented for

Him, because He basically didn't build personal relationships with people outside of His circle of disciples.

6. But, in spite of the bond that He shared with Lazarus and his sisters, Jesus did not immediately rush to Bethany to see about His sick friend, as requested. On the contrary, He stayed where He was for two more whole days before even acknowledging the situation.

7. Then, finally, He said to His disciples, "We need to go back to Judea. I'm ready now."

8. "But Teacher," they said, "just the other day when You were there, the local people were attempting to stone You to death! Do You think it's a good idea to go back there right now?"

9. Jesus answered them, "Are there not twelve hours in the day? Whoever walks around in the daytime does not stumble, because they see everything by this world's light.

10. "It is when people try to walk at night that they stumble, for they have no light for their path."

11. After saying this, He continued, "Our friend Lazarus has fallen asleep and I need to go there and wake him up."

12. His disciples replied, "Lord, if he is sick, it is good for him to get as much rest as possible. Sleep is therapeutic...the more he gets, the sooner he will get better."

13. But Jesus was speaking of something else entirely. Even though He didn't want to say it, and even though He had said that it wouldn't happen, Jesus knew within Himself that Lazarus had died. But his disciples didn't discern this and thought that He was referring to natural sleep.

14. So He spelled it out for them: "Lazarus is dead;

15. and, for your sake, I am actually glad that I was not there to prevent it from happening so that you may

begin to believe on a whole new level. Now let us go to him."

16. Then Thomas (whose Greek name was Didymus), demonstrated how clueless they all were by chiming in with a bizarrely random and irrelevant suggestion. "Let us also go, that we may die with him!" he said. No one even responded to this strange response to Jesus' announcement that He was going to raise Lazarus up; they just started on their journey.

17. Upon His arrival, Jesus discovered that Lazarus had already been in the tomb for four days.

18. Now Bethany was less than two miles from Jerusalem,

19. and many people from there had come to visit Mary and Martha to comfort them in the loss of their beloved brother.

20. When Martha heard that Jesus was approaching the house, she went out to meet Him on the way. Mary, on the other hand, just stayed indoors.

21. "Lord," Martha said to Jesus, "where have You been? If You had just come when we called for You, my brother would be alive right now!

22. "But even though I am brokenhearted that You ignored our message, I know that God will give You whatever You ask."

23. Without apology Jesus said to her, "Martha, your brother will rise again."

24. She answered Him, "Yes, I know that eventually he will rise again in the resurrection, but that's little consolation to us in the here and now."

25. Jesus said to her, "You need to stop thinking of the resurrection as an event and begin to see it as a person, and that person is Me! I am the Resurrection and the Life! Whoever believes in Me will live, in spite of the fact that they experience the rite of passage called death.

26. "Whoever lives by believing in Me will not even be

affected by death. Do you believe what I'm telling you?"

27. "Yes, Lord," she replied, "I do believe that You are the Messiah, the Son of God who has come into our world!"

28. After she had said this, she went back to the house to speak privately with her sister. "Our Friend, the Teacher is here," she said, "and He is asking for you."

29. When Mary heard this, she gathered up her courage and went out to meet Him.

30. At this point, Jesus had not yet entered the village but was still at the place where Martha had met Him.

31. When the local people who had been with Mary in the house, comforting her, saw how quickly she got up from her place of mourning and went out, they followed her. They assumed that she was going back to the tomb and they wanted to be there for her.

32. But when Mary reached the place where Jesus was and saw Him face to face, she became overwhelmed with emotion and fell, prostrate, at His feet. Seeing Him brought it all home for her...the sorrow...the anger...the disappointment...the pain. "Lord," she sobbed, "if You had been here, my brother would not have died."

33. Mary's obvious grief affected the people who were with her, because they all started crying, as well. When Jesus saw Mary and all of her friends weeping so pitifully, it really hit Him hard. The whole scenario touched Him on so many levels that all He could do was deeply groan in His spirit. When it came to ministry, Jesus was usually able to keep some emotional distance between Him and those who needed Him, but this was different. This really troubled Him.

34. "Where have you laid him?" He asked. "Come and see, Lord," they replied, and they led Him to Lazarus' burial site.

35. When Jesus finally saw the tomb, He just broke down and wept. A few days before, He had boldly prophesied that Lazarus' sickness was not going to end in death, and now He had every intention of supernaturally reversing time and making that prophecy come true. Only a short while earlier, He had even announced to Martha, very authoritatively, that He was the Resurrection and the Life. But when He experienced with His own two eyes the harsh reality of seeing a close friend's grave, He so identified with the human condition that all He could do was cry. His immediate reaction to the sight was not that of "the Resurrection and the Life," but that of a completely human being who was dealing with a sense of loss on a very personal level.

36. When the people saw Him crying, they were very moved and said, "Look at that...see how much He loved him!"

37. But some of them said, "Then why didn't He prevent this from happening? He can open the eyes of the blind; why couldn't He save the life of His own friend?"

38. Hearing all this talk only forced Jesus to groan even more deeply in His spirit. His human nature was competing here with His divine nature in a very profound way. The Son of God was ready to perform a miracle, but the Son of Man just wanted and needed to grieve for His friend. But, in spite of this inner conflict, He approached the tomb, which was really just a cave with a stone laid across the entrance, and said,

39. "Take away the stone." "But Lord," Martha protested, "his body has been in there for four days and by now is decaying and putting off a bad odor. Please, just let him be."

40. But at this point Jesus was neither groaning nor weeping. And with great conviction He declared to

her, "Have I not told you that if you believe, you will see the very glory of God?"

41. Martha said nothing, but His words so dominated the atmosphere that they motivated some of the people to remove the stone. Then He looked up and said, "Father, I thank You that You have heard Me.

42. "And that goes without saying, because I know that You always hear Me; but I am speaking this out loud for the benefit of these standing here so that they may believe that You sent Me."

43. After saying these words, Jesus called in a loud voice, "Lazarus, come out of there!"

44. And in virtually no time, that dead man came out alive! His hands and feet were wrapped in linen strips and a cloth was tied around his face, so Jesus said to the stunned people standing there, "Now, take off his grave clothes and let him go!"

45. Naturally, many of the people who had come to visit Mary, and had seen what Jesus did there, easily put their faith in Him at that point.

46. But some of them made it their business to go to the Pharisees to tell them what Jesus had done *this* time.

47. Then the chief priests and the Pharisees called a meeting of the entire Sanhedrin court to discuss the matter of this Miracle Worker. They said, "We've got to do something about Jesus of Nazareth, but what? He not only continues to perform these signs and wonders, but they seem to be getting increasingly more elaborate and dramatic!

48. "If we don't put a stop to His influence and magic, the whole nation will eventually believe in Him. And if that happens, the Romans will get involved and will come and suppress us and take away our holy place...our temple...our city...our nation. He could potentially ruin everything for us!"

49. But one of them, Caiaphas, who was the high priest that year, spoke up and said, "You know nothing at

all!

50. "You need to realize that it is better for all of us that one man die for the people, than that the whole nation perish."

51. He did not say this on his own; he was not self-motivated. But, as the high priest that year, he was authorized to prophesy, and so he prophesied that Jesus would die for the nation.

52. And not only for the Jewish nation, but also for the purpose of uniting into one body the children of God who have been scattered to all the nations of the earth.

53. So, from that day, they began to plot together how they could take His life from Him.

54. From then on, Jesus no longer publicly moved among those who could be influenced by the Jewish religious leaders. Instead, He withdrew to an area near the wilderness, to a village called Ephraim, where He stayed with His disciples.

55. When it was almost time for Passover, many went up from the country to Jerusalem for the traditional cleansing ceremony that was required for it.

56. They kept looking for Jesus there. People gathered in the temple courts and asked one another, "Have you heard anything about Jesus? Do you know if He is coming to the festival at all?"

57. Everyone was interested in Him for one reason or another. But they all knew that the chief priests and Pharisees had given strict orders that if anyone knew of Jesus' whereabouts, they were to report to them immediately because there was a warrant for His arrest.

Chapter 12

1. Six days before the Feast of Passover, Jesus went back to Bethany where He had raised Lazarus from

death.

2. His main reason for returning to the village was that Martha had prepared a big meal to honor Him and to show her appreciation for Lazarus' miracle. So she served up a great feast and Lazarus sat right next to Him at the table.

3. It was a beautiful time of celebration and, after the meal, Mary brought in a jar of very expensive aromatic oils with which she anointed and massaged Jesus' feet. Then she wiped them with her hair and the sweet smell of the perfumed oils filled the whole house.

4. But one of his disciples, Judas Iscariot, who was already having thoughts of betraying Him, objected:

5. "Why wasn't this perfume sold and the money given to the poor? It was worth a year's wages...a small fortune."

6. He didn't say this because he cared about the poor, but because he was a thief. Even though he had been entrusted with the office of treasurer and accountant for Jesus' ministry, he was in the habit of helping himself to the money whenever he needed it for his own personal use.

7. "Leave her alone," Jesus replied. "She has done this in preparation for My burial. And, furthermore, you need to realize the truth about the poor. Even if you gave them all the money from the sale of this expensive oil and more, it would not eradicate their poverty. Only a change in their mindset can do that.

8. "In other words, you'll always have the poor with you, but you won't always have Me."

9. Now word got out that He was back in town, so a great number of people came to see Him. And, of course, everyone was extremely curious to see Lazarus, the man who had been raised from the dead.

10. So the chief priests plotted to put Lazarus to death, also.

11. He was added to their hit list because, on account of him and his amazing miracle, many of the local people were leaving their traditional faith and believing in Jesus.

12. The next day, a huge crowd assembled in Jerusalem for the Passover Feast. When they heard that Jesus was coming there for the festival,

13. they took palm branches and went out to meet Him, loudly shouting to Him, "Hosanna! Blessed is He who comes in God's name. Blessed is the King of Israel!"

14. But Jesus found a young donkey and sat on it, to fulfill what was written:

15. "Don't be afraid people of Israel. Look, your King is coming, sitting on a donkey's colt."

16. At first, His disciples didn't get it at all. But after Jesus was glorified, they remembered all this and realized that everything had happened exactly as the Scriptures had said it would.

17. Those in the crowd who had seen Jesus raise Lazarus from the dead, were talking about it incessantly. And as they kept recounting the story over and over, the excitement from the whole thing just spread like wildfire among the people.

18. And that's why the crowd was so huge and noisy that day. The whole town was so electrified with the news of Jesus' power and ability, that a kind of mania had set in among them.

19. So when the Pharisees saw what was happening, they said to one another, "This thing is out of control! Look! The entire world has gone after Jesus!"

20. Now there were some Greeks among those who went up to celebrate and worship at the Feast.

21. And they approached Philip (who was from Bethsaida in Galilee), with a request. "Sir," they said, "we've got to see this Jesus that everyone is talking about!"

22. Philip went to tell Andrew and, in turn, Andrew and

Philip told Jesus.

23. But Jesus answered them, saying, "The hour has come for the Son of Man to be glorified.

24. "And this is the truth that you need to grasp: Unless a kernel of wheat falls to the ground and dies, it remains only a single seed. But if it dies, the course of nature sees to it that it is then able to produce innumerable seeds!

25. "Those who love their natural life more than their spiritual life will lose their natural life. But those who let go of this natural life will walk in the fullness of eternal life…a life in the now…and they will have it here and in the next dimension.

26. "All those who want to be My disciples must come and follow Me because My servants need to be where I am. And if they follow Me into full comprehension of eternal life, the Father will honor them.

27. "Now My soul is troubled...My inner conflict is intense...but what can I do about it? I can't say, 'Father, save Me from this hour of trial and agony,' because this is what I came for!

28. "At this point, all I can say is 'Father, glorify Your name through this!'" Just then a voice from the eternal realm manifested into the natural dimension and said, "I have glorified it by sending You there, and I will glorify it again by receiving You back here."

29. Everyone in the crowd heard it, but some of them dismissed it as nothing but a clap of thunder. Others surmised that an angel had spoken to Him.

30. But Jesus said, "This voice did not speak for My benefit, but for yours.

31. "Now the crisis point of this world has arrived, and now the administration of the so-called 'prince of this world' has come to an end. The one who has presented himself as the evil genius of this dimension is finished...finally cast down and cast out.

32. "And now begins the new era of My reign, the time for Me to be lifted up. And if I am lifted up from the earth, first in humiliation on the cross and then in triumph on the throne of My kingdom, I will personally draw all of humanity...every ethnicity, culture, and people group...to Myself!"

33. He said this to show the kind of death He was going to die, because a large part of the horror of crucifixion was the public humiliation and exposure of it. Jesus would be crucified naked, and elevated to a level where all could see Him, so that He could bear the shame of every individual's sin consciousness. The Romans "lifted up" their victims on crosses to make public spectacles of them – the idea being that the visibility of those executed would serve as a deterrent to crime and rebellion. But Jesus would be lifted up so that everyone, everywhere, could identify Him, and identify *with* Him, so that they could see Him high above the crowd and be able to know where and how to find Him from any place on the earth.

34. But the crowd spoke up and said, "We have heard from the law that the Christ will remain forever, so how can you say, 'The Son of Man must be lifted up'? And who is this 'Son of Man' that you keep talking about, anyway?"

35. So Jesus said to them, "You will only have the Light in this way a little while longer. You must walk while you have the Light; walk before darkness overtakes you. Those who walk in the dark have no idea where they are going.

36. "Believe in the Light while you have the Light; your faith in the Light will cause you to become sons and daughters of the Light, beings of light who are filled with light." When He had finished speaking, Jesus left and hid Himself from them.

37. Even after Jesus had performed so many amazing signs and wonders in their presence – right before

their very eyes – they still would not believe in Him.

38. And this phenomenon (the fact that they couldn't see Him because of the blindness of their religion, even though He revealed Himself to them) fulfilled Isaiah's words: "Lord, who has believed our message, and to whom has the mighty, muscled arm of the Lord been revealed?"

39. This explains why they could not believe, because Isaiah also said,

40. "He has blinded their eyes and hardened their hearts, so they can neither see with their eyes nor understand with their hearts, nor turn around and face Me so that I could heal them."

41. Isaiah said this because he saw Jesus' glory in the eternal now and spoke about Him in the dimension of time. And he prophesied these things because it was necessary for Israel, as a nation, to reject Jesus as being their Messiah, so that the gospel would be forced to become global, finding its universal manifestation in the diverse dimension of the Holy Spirit.

42. Yet at the same time, many, even among the religious leaders, believed in Him. But, because of the Pharisees, they would not openly confess it for fear they would be put out of the synagogue.

43. For they loved religious approval and human glory more than the glory of the true God.

44. Then Jesus cried out with a loud voice, "Those who believe in Me do not believe in Me only, but in the One who sent Me!

45. "When they look at Me, they are really looking at the One who sent Me here!

46. "I have come into this physical world to light it up – to illuminate it with the brightness of My shining truth – so that no one who believes in Me should continue to live in darkness.

47. "As for those who hear My words but do not observe

to do them, I do not judge them because I did not come into this dimension to judge the world. My only reason for coming here was to save the world, the *whole* world.

48. "But anyone who consistently rejects My teachings already has his judge. My very message itself will ultimately convict him.

49. "And the reason I say this is that I have never spoken on My own authority, but the Father who sent Me has commanded Me to say everything that I have said.

50. "And I know that His commandment activates the full potential of eternal life. So, whatever I speak, you can be sure that I am saying exactly what My Father has told Me to say – no more, no less – My words are in perfect accordance with His instructions."

Chapter 13

1. It was right before the Feast of Passover, and Jesus knew that the time had come for Him to physically leave the earthly dimension and return, full-time, to the spirit realm to be with His Father in the now. And having loved His own who were in the world, He continued to love them right up to the very end of His existence as the Word made flesh. He loved those twelve men with an intense and unfailing love, as much as any human being could possibly love another. He didn't simply have divine affection for them as an almighty Creator would have for His creation; His connection with them was more complex...more than that of God benevolently loving mankind. He actually cared for them with the very vulnerable, heart-felt emotion of a man who enjoyed their company and depended on them as His partners in the ministry. They were His friends, they were His confidants, they were His brothers, they were His

sons. They had worked together, prayed together, fished together, changed people's lives together. They had all become a part of each other.

2.   But as the evening meal progressed, Judas became increasingly adversarial toward Jesus in his attitude, giving in to his dark side in a way that made it seem as though the devil had entered him and had prompted him to betray Jesus. On another occasion, Jesus had referred to Judas as a devil (which simply means adversary), and now His prophetic words were coming to pass.

3.   But Jesus, being completely confident in the fact that God had put Him in charge of everything that was happening and everything that was about to happen, was not intimidated by what was going on inside Judas' mind. He was focused on the knowledge that, in the same way that He had come from God, He was about to return to God.

4.   So He got up from the table, stripped down completely, and wrapped a towel around His waist. In so doing, He girded Himself in the manner that servant boys did at that time when they waited on houseguests.

5.   Then He poured water into a basin and began to humbly and deliberately wash His disciples' feet, drying them with the towel that He had wrapped around His waist.

6.   But when He got to Simon Peter, Peter objected, saying, "Lord, surely You do not intend on washing *my* feet!"

7.   Jesus replied, "You aren't able to comprehend what I'm doing right now, but later it will make perfect sense to you."

8.   "No!" Peter said emphatically. "It's not right. I will never permit You to be subservient to me in this way. I absolutely will not allow You to ever wash my feet!" Jesus answered, "Let Me put it to you this way,

Peter. Unless I wash you, you have no part with Me."

9. "All right, then," Peter finally said. "If that's the way it is, if it is that important, then go ahead and do it, but don't just wash my feet...wash my hands and my head, as well!"

10. But Jesus answered him, saying, "Those who have had a bath only need to wash their feet after walking on a dirty floor, because the rest of their body is clean. This act is symbolic in that you, as a group, are clean, but not every one of you."

11. He said this because He knew who was going to betray Him, and that was why He said that not every one of them was clean.

12. When He had completed washing the feet of each disciple, He put His clothes back on and returned to where He had been sitting at the table. Then He asked them, "Do you have any idea why I have done what I just did?

13. "Let Me explain: You call Me 'Teacher' and 'Lord,' and it is appropriate that you do so because that is what I am.

14. "But the point is this: Now that I, your Lord and Teacher, have washed your feet, you should also serve one another in this same way. You should take every opportunity to wash one another's feet just as I have washed yours.

15. "I have set the example for you – the example of unconditional love, of covering one another, of serving one another, and honoring one another. This is a kingdom principle, and you should continue to do for one another as I have done for you,

16. because the truth is that servants are not greater than their master, and those who deliver a message are not greater than the one who sent them to deliver it.

17. "And now that I have demonstrated these principles to you, you are responsible for them, and you will be blessed if you do them.

18. "And you need to know that what I am saying applies to every one of you. I know those that I have chosen, and I never second-guess My choices. But what is happening, even as I speak, is the fulfillment of the Scripture that says 'He who shared My bread with Me has lifted up his heel against Me.'

19. "I am prepared for this, but I am telling you about it now, before it happens, so that when it comes to pass you will have another reason to believe that I am who I am.

20. "Always remember how this truth works in this dimension: Whoever accepts anyone that I send, ultimately accepts Me, and, likewise, whoever accepts Me accepts the One who sent Me."

21. But as soon as He said this, the reality of what was happening dawned on His human nature, and He became troubled and depressed in His spirit. The God part of Him was fully in control of the situation, even emotionally detached from it, in a way. But the part of Him that was a man – the part that loved Judas as a friend and a brother – suddenly cried out in sorrow, "The painful truth is that one of you sitting right here is going to betray Me!"

22. His disciples were so dumbfounded at this that they just stared at one another in disbelief. No one knew what to say.

23. But one of them, the one known as the disciple that Jesus loved, was reclining so close to Jesus that he was actually leaning on Him.

24. And Simon Peter motioned to this disciple and said to him, "Lean in a little closer so that He can whisper to you who He's talking about."

25. So, leaning back even closer into Jesus' personal space, he asked, "Lord, who is it? Who is going to betray You?"

26. Jesus responded to him, saying, "The one to whom I give this piece of bread after I have dipped it into the

dish." Then He dipped the bread and handed it to Judas, the son of Simon Iscariot.

27. As soon as Judas took the bread, a sense of darkness overtook him and he completely surrendered to the devilish plan to betray Jesus. And, being fully aware of what had just taken place in Judas' heart, Jesus said to him, "Don't put off what you are going to do any longer; go ahead and get it over with quickly."

28. But the disciples were so in denial of what was actually transpiring in that moment, that not one of them was able to understand what Jesus was talking about. It was too unthinkable for them to grasp that anyone in that room, including Judas, was capable of actually turning against Jesus.

29. So, since Judas was in charge of the finances, they just assumed that Jesus was telling him to buy what was needed to celebrate the festival or to give something to the poor. That was the end of it as far as they were concerned.

30. But nothing was ever the same after Judas took that bread from Jesus, and they both knew it. There were no other words that needed to be said, so he just got up and quietly went out into the shadows of the night.

31. As soon as the door closed behind him, Jesus turned to the remaining disciples and said, "Now the Son of Man is glorified, and God is glorified in Him.

32. "And if God is glorified in Him, He will glorify the Son in Himself, and He will glorify Him in the now.

33. "Listen, My sons; I am only going to be with you a little while longer. You will look for Me, and as I told the people in the temple so I tell you now, 'Where I am going you cannot come.'

34. "So this is what I need to leave with you – these are My last words to you – what I want, more than anything, for you to remember. I have given you many instructions and insights during our time together, but here is the new commandment, the new

order, the thing that is superior to every other thing, in a word: LOVE ONE ANOTHER. In the way that I have loved you, so you must love one another. Do you understand?

35. "You see, this is the only way that people will know that you are My disciples. Your love for one another is the solitary thing that will validate My message in the long run – not the miracles, not the signs and wonders, not the teaching – but your unconditional love for each other. It is not optional."

36. Simon Peter asked Him, "Lord, where exactly are You going?" Jesus answered him, "Peter, where I am going, you cannot go. It is not possible for you to follow Me there now, but you will be able to follow Me there later."

37. But Peter said, "I don't want to wait! Why can't I follow You now? Don't You realize how important You are to me? I mean, I would lay down my very life for You!"

38. Then Jesus answered, "I know that you think you really mean that, but the truth is that you will disown Me – you will actually deny that you ever even knew Me – three times before the rooster crows tomorrow morning.

Chapter 14

1. "But don't let your heart be troubled about this, Peter, and that goes for the rest of you, as well. Just believe in God and believe also in Me, and you will survive what is about to happen to all of us.

2. "Even though you will definitely deny Me three times, there will still always be a room for you in the Father's house – a room with your name on the door. And that room represents your secure and unique place of effectiveness in ministry, your guarantee of

personally staying in good standing with Me, regardless of what you do in the next few hours, or for the rest of your life, for that matter. If this were not the case, you can be sure that I would tell you. In fact, I am going to the cross to personally prepare this place for you in My purpose.

3.   "And if I go to prepare this room for you, I will come back from the grave and personally receive you to Myself...move you into the Father's house to live with Me indefinitely...so that where I am, you may be, also. In this way, you will never doubt your eternal place with Me again and will never again succumb to any pressure put upon you to deny Me.

4.   "And really, you already know in your heart where I am going and how to get there for yourself."

5.   Thomas spoke up and said, "Lord, don't take for granted that we know where You are going. We don't! How can we know the way to the Father's house if we don't fully understand what and where it is?"

6.   Jesus said, to him, "I am the Way, and the Truth, and the Life. Ultimately, no one can find his or her way to the Father's house without Me personally taking them there. There are many paths one may take to find Me, but I am the Way.

7.   "By knowing Me, you are able to know the Father, so from now on, realize that you know Him...you actually know God and have seen Him in Me."

8.   Philip, said to Him, "Lord, just show us the Father, that's all we ask. Only seeing Him will really satisfy us."

9.   Jesus replied, "Did you not hear what I just said, Philip? How could I have been with you all this time and you still not be able to recognize Me? I'm telling you again: anyone who has seen Me has already seen the Father. How can you so ignorantly say then, 'Show us the Father'?

10. "Do you not believe that I am in the Father and that the Father is in Me?

11. "By now you should easily believe that the Father and I are completely integrated, if for no other reason than because of the wonderworks that I perform.

12. "And I'll tell you something else, something really important, and it's the absolute truth, even though you may find it hard to believe. Those who believe in Me will do the very same works that I have been doing, and they will actually do even greater things than I have done because I am going to be reunited with the Father in the eternal realm.

13. "And I will do whatever you ask in My name, or on the authority of My reputation, so that the Father may be glorified in the Son.

14. "We will walk in such harmony that you may ask Me for anything in My name, and I will do it.

15. "If you really love Me, keep these commands of Mine.

16. "And I will ask the Father to send you another Helper, just as He sent Me to you. And this Helper will be your Comforter, Advocate, Intercessor, Standby...and He will never have to leave you as I have to leave you now. He will be with you indefinitely...forever.

17. "He is the Spirit of Truth, and the world at large cannot comprehend or accept Him at this point because it has no perception of His reality. But you already know Him because He has been living *with* you, and as soon as I am released from this physical manifestation, He will begin to live *in* you.

18. "Just because I will no longer be seen by you in this incarnation, does not mean that you will be orphaned by Me. I will come right back to you as My Spirit-self.

19. "In a few hours the world will no longer see this flesh-man, but you will still see Me with your spiritual eyes. You will not be limited any longer to

only seeing this Jesus, but you will be freed and released to see this Christ! And because I will transcend and outlive the physical, you will also transcend and outlive the physical.

20. "When all this comes together for you, you will realize that I am in My Father, and you are in Me, and I am in you…all together…all connected…all one!

21. "And whoever holds on to My commands and does them, proves that they love Me. And those who love Me will experience the reality of the Father's love for them, and it will ultimately reveal to them who I really am and who I have been all along."

22. Then Judas (not Judas Iscariot) said, "But, Lord, what is the point of revealing Yourself to us if You're not going to reveal Yourself to the whole world?"

23. Jesus said to him, "Anyone who loves Me will obey My teaching and precepts, and they will experience the fullness of the Father's love. In this way, they will become the dwelling place of the Father in Me, or Me in the Father; in other words, those who are obedient will become the house of God.

24. "But anyone who does not love Me will not obey My teaching, so they will not enjoy this privilege. So, in answer to your question, Judas, the revelation is in the obedience, and anyone in the world who obeys can have the same revelation of Me that you have. These words are not My own – they are the words of the Father who sent Me.

25. "I have told you as much as I can while I am still with you in the physical realm.

26. "But this Advocate/Helper that I'm telling you about – the Holy Spirit, whom the Father will send in My behalf – will teach you all of this. He will remind you of everything that I have said to you and will make it all make sense to you. So don't be unsettled about these mysteries. I don't want to leave you in a state of turmoil.

27. "Peace I leave with you; I'm talking about My own, personal sense of peace, wholeness and well-being; I'm actually transferring it to you. You see, My peace is unlike the peace that comes from this realm...the peace that is reactionary and temporal, dependent on outward circumstances to determine its strength and presence. My peace is other-worldly... settled, absolute, causing you to be in harmony with your whole life – past, present, and future – and ultimately with the whole of creation. It will empower you to refuse to let your heart (your inner world) become troubled, agitated, or upset, no matter what is happening around you, and you can be fearless because you will be at peace with the Father, with yourself, and with the universe.

28. "At this point, you should be comfortable with the idea that I am going away, because I have told you that I would be back. If you love Me properly and unselfishly, you will celebrate the fact that I am going to the Father, because the Father is greater and mightier than even I am.

29. "This is another thing that I have told you before it happens, so that when it comes to pass, you will believe.

30. "But I will not say much more to you from this point on because it is time for the final conflict between light and darkness to be consummated, and words are unnecessary now. In this way, the one who claims to be the prince of this world is coming to Me, but I have nothing more to say to him. He has no place in My consciousness.

31. "But he has a purpose to serve, and I will allow it. His coming to Me will cause the world to understand that I love the Father and do exactly what My Father has commanded Me, because everything that I have done and am about to do is because of My relationship to My Father. Now, I have a few more

things to say to you, but let's leave this place. I will say the rest while we walk."

Chapter 15

1. Then He said to them, "I am the True Vine – the Real, Authentic Vine that produces life in this world – and My Father is the Gardener and Vinedresser.
2. "Any branch in Me that is not fruitful or productive, He purifies and cleans.
3. "But you have already been cleansed, thoroughly made clean through the word that I have spoken to you.
4. "Stay connected to Me in your mind and attitude, and I will continue to produce life in you. In the same way that a branch can't bear fruit by itself, but only by being joined to the vine, you can't bear fruit in your life without staying connected to Me in your consciousness.
5. "I really want you to understand this: I am the Vine, you are the branches. Whoever stays connected to Me, mentally and spiritually, will bear much fruit and will continue to be productive. But disconnected from Me, you can do nothing.
6. "Whoever intentionally separates himself or herself from Me just dries up and withers like a dead branch that is only useful as firewood.
7. "But if you continue to stay mentally and spiritually connected to Me, and if My words, My teachings, My concepts, become a vital part of your everyday life, then you will have the confidence to ask for whatever you want and your desires will be granted.
8. "In this way, My Father is honored. He is exalted through your fruitfulness, and only those who are fruitful and productive are My true disciples.
9. "You need to realize that I have loved you with the

same intensity with which the Father has loved Me, so remain faithful to My unfailing love for you.

10. "If you keep My commandments, you will maintain intimacy with Me. You will be confident in My love for you, as I am confident in the Father's love for Me. Your obedience will reinforce our covenant of love.

11. "And I am telling you all of this for one reason: that My joy may remain in you and that your joy may be full. In other words, I want you to be as completely happy as I am!

12. "And this is My essential and ultimate commandment that will bring you joy and happiness: that you love one another in the same way that I have loved and do love you, unconditionally, completely, wholly, eternally.

13. "And the utmost test of love is this: that a person lays down his or her life for his or her friends.

14. "You show that you are My friends by keeping My commandments, especially this main one.

15. "I think of you as My friends, not as My servants, because a servant does not necessarily know what his master is doing. But I call you friends, because I have made known to you everything that I have heard from My Father through the intimate, everyday conversation that friends have.

16. "You did not choose Me. I chose you, just like you were, and I sent you out to produce fruit in your life and ministry – the kind of fruit that will never spoil, but will last eternally.

17. "And again, I can't stress enough how important this commandment is: LOVE ONE ANOTHER!

18. "If you find that the promoters of this world-system hate you, don't take it personally. Remember that they hated Me first, and their intense dislike is more about Me than it is about you.

19. "If you blindly followed the rules of the religious world-system, its proponents would love you. But

you are non-conformists and iconoclasts like Me, so the people who feel threatened by you will hate you. People who do not walk in the light always hate and fight what they don't understand.

20. "So don't forget this: A servant is not greater than his master. If people mistreat Me, they will mistreat you. It comes with the territory. But if they have done what *I* told them, then they will do what *you* tell them to do.

21. "Basically, people will do to you exactly what they did to Me, because you belong to Me and they don't know the One who sent Me.

22. "If I hadn't been so open and candid with them, they would not be guilty of the sin of closed-minded unbelief. But now they have no excuse; from now on there is no excuse for anyone refusing to walk in the light.

23. "But the bottom line is that whoever hates Me, hates My Father, also.

24. "You surely must realize that I have done things that no one else has ever done, and I have done them right before the eyes of the general public. If I had not been so visible – if I had not made the truth so accessible – they would not be guilty. But many of them have seen and heard it all and still hate both Me and My Father.

25. "That is why the Scriptures are true when they say, 'The people hated Me for no good reason.'

26. "But when the Helper comes, whom I will send from the Father, He will be revealed as the Spirit of Truth, and He will tell you all about Me. He will fill in all the blanks for you and will make all of this make sense to your spirit and to your mind.

27. "Then you will be empowered to also easily tell others about Me, because you have been with Me from the beginning and you will know exactly what to say.

Chapter 16

1. "I am telling you all of these things before I leave you so that you will not be afraid and will not fall apart when things get rough.

2. "You need to be prepared for this: The religious people are going to evict you from their synagogues and meeting places. In fact, the time will come when some of them will become so self-righteous that they will be capable of killing you, thinking that they are doing God a service in doing so. Religion will make them so blindly intolerant that they will actually think that murdering you will be their way of doing God a favor!

3. "They will do these things only because they don't know Me and, therefore, do not know the Father.

4. "I am saying this to you now so that, when it happens, you will remember My words and will not be unprepared for it. I haven't told you these things before now because I've been with you every day, and I knew that I could take care of everything in person.

5. "But now I am going back to the Father – back into the eternal now – and yet not one of you seems to be curious about where I am going.

6. "You are too preoccupied with your own personal sadness about what you perceive to be something wonderful that is coming to an end.

7. "But you need to realize that this is really a new beginning for us all! It is to your advantage that I go away, because if I do not leave this fleshly incarnation, the Holy Spirit cannot come to you. But if I leave this realm, I will personally be able to send Him to you.

8. "And when He comes, He will show everyone around the world the truth about sin and God's justice and

about how judgment works.

9. "The Spirit will show them that they were wrong about Me – that it was a sin to reject Me and not believe in Me.

10. "He will show them the truth about righteousness, and they will be able to understand it then because I will be with the Father, and you won't see Me in this present incarnation again.

11. "And He will show them the truth about judgment, because God has already judged the so-called ruler of this world.

12. "I really have so many more things to say to you, but I think that you are already saturated and a little overwhelmed with all this.

13. "But don't worry about it. When the Spirit of Truth is finally revealed, He will guide you into all the truth that there is. He will not speak on His own and tell you something different than what I have told you. He will only tell you what He has heard from Me, and He will give you the insight to know what is ahead so that you can actually see into the future.

14. "The Spirit will glorify Me because He will take My message and make it global and universal. And He will declare it to you, directly.

15. "Everything that the Father has is Mine. That is why it is so important that the Spirit takes My message and integrates it into your consciousness.

16. "In just a short while you will not be able to see Me with the natural eye, but then you will be able to perceive Me by the Spirit because I am returning to the Father in the now."

17. Then some of His disciples really began to react to His words. "What does He mean by saying, 'In a little while you won't be able to see Me with the natural eye, but then you will see Me by the Spirit?' Why does He say, 'I am going to the Father'?"

18. They also asked, "What in the world does He mean

by 'a little while'? We do not understand His mysterious words, at all!"

19. Jesus was fully aware of their confused curiosity, so He said to them, "Are you asking one another what I meant by saying, 'In a little while you will see Me no more, and then after a while you will see Me again?'

20. "Here's the truth about that: You will initially weep and mourn while the slaves to this world-system rejoice. You will grieve, but then your grief will be turned into joy!

21. "When a woman gives birth to a child, she has pain in her labor and delivery. But that pain is put into perspective when the baby is born, to the point that she seems to forget the physical, altogether. The joy that the baby brings is so much greater than any suffering that it may have caused, that the hardship of labor becomes completely irrelevant and insignificant.

22. "So it is with you. You are about to feel your own pains of labor in grieving over My departure from this fleshly manifestation. But I will see you again when I am 'born' in the person of the Holy Spirit, and then you will have so much joy that you will forget this present sorrow, completely. And when that happens, no one will ever be able to take your joy away from you!

23. "There is a new era coming, and in that era you will no longer ask Me anything. You will ask God the Father, directly, and He will give you whatever you ask for in My name or on behalf of My reputation.

24. "Until now you have not prayed with this mindset, but now you will be able to ask, and you will receive. And I want you to do this simply because it will make your joy complete; the miracle of answered prayer will grant you unsurpassed happiness.

25. "I have been speaking to you in parables and allegories, but the time is about to arrive when I will

speak to you plainly about the Father. You are ready for real communication.

26. "When that time comes, you will be able to pray in My name, or on the strength of My reputation, and your words will go directly to the Father's ears. It will not even be necessary for Me to speak to the Father on your behalf, because you will already be in Me and I will be in Him.

27. "For the Father has a loving relationship with you – person to person…face to face – because you have loved Me and have believed that I came out of the Father.

28. "I came from the Father in the now and entered the dimension of space and time – or the natural world as you know it – and now I am leaving this dimension and going back to the Father…back to the now."

29. Then Jesus' disciples said, "Ah! Now we are beginning to understand! It seems as if You are suddenly speaking plainly to us – not in parables or mysteries or figures of speech. It's as if a veil has been lifted.

30. "We are at peace with the fact that You clearly know everything, including where You are going, and You don't need to be questioned any further. We get it: You really did come from God."

31. Jesus answered them, "Now do you believe?

32. "The time will come, in fact it is already here, when all of you will be temporarily scattered. You will all panic and leave Me alone, but I will not really be alone because the Father is always with Me.

33. "I have told you these things so that, in Me, you may have real peace and confident serenity. Now don't be naïve to the fact that, in the world, you will have trouble; it is a given. But, take heart! You can celebrate and live a joyful life, regardless of any circumstances in your life, because I have completely overcome the trouble of the world and have set the

example to show how you can overcome it, as well!"

Chapter 17

1.   After Jesus had finished speaking to His disciples, He looked up toward the infinite sky and said, "Father, the time has come for You to bring glory to Your Son so that Your Son may glorify You.

2.   "You have granted Him full authority over all the people of the earth, and You have given them to Him so that He might give them all eternal life.

3.   "And this fulfills the purpose of eternal life, that they may know You, the only true God, and Jesus Christ, the manifestation of Your physical presence on the earth.

4.   "I brought glory to You in this dimension by doing everything that You told Me to do.

5.   "And now, Father, bring Me back into the eternal now so that I may exist in the glory that We shared before the world began.

6.   "I have told these men who have followed Me all about You. Their perception was limited, having been shaped by the current world's system, but You gave them to Me and now they have been freed from the smallness of their previous mindset by obeying Your word.

7.   "They know that everything that I have came from You.

8.   "I just told them exactly what You told Me, and it convinced them that I came from You and that You sent Me here.

9.   "Right now I am not praying for the whole world, but for those whom You have given to be My followers, because they know that they belong to You.

10.   "All that I have is Yours, and all that You have is Mine, and the glory of that connection has now

included them in its manifestation.

11. "I will no longer remain in this dimension or in this physical incarnation, but *they* are still in the physical realm of space and time. I am returning to the eternal now to be reintegrated with and in You, but I pray, Holy Father, that You keep, through Your name, those whom You have given Me. I pray that, even though they continue to live and move in the physical world, they will be able to transcend its finite limitations and be one with each other, even as We are.

12. "While I was with them in the physical world, I kept them safe and intact in Your name. I carefully guarded them, and not one of them was lost to My circle of influence, except for that one who just seemed bent on destruction. But his rebellion only served to fulfill the Scriptures.

13. "I am on My way back into the eternal now, but I want to say these things while I am still in this physical incarnation. If I say these things as the Son of Man, it will make it possible for them to also say these kinds of things so that they can know the joy of being manifested as Sons of God.

14. "I have told them Your message, but they are hated by those mental prisoners of the world-system, because they don't belong to that system in any way, just as I don't.

15. "Father, I don't ask that you take My followers out of the world, because it would defeat the entire purpose of My coming here if You should allow them to become escapists. I only pray that they be kept safe from the phantom menace.

16. "They are misfits in this world – strangers to its present mindset – just like Me.

17. "So let them find shelter in the truth of Your word; it is the only place where they can live now that they have been with Me.

18. "As You sent Me into this dimension, I am sending them into it – into the fullness of it.

19. "I have given Myself completely for their sake – becoming absolutely absorbed into them – so that they may become absolutely absorbed into the truth.

20. "But I do not pray for these alone...these who know Me as I am, here and now. But I pray for those everywhere and in every dimension of time, including those in the future, who will ultimately believe in Me through their witness and their word.

21. "And I pray that they all may be one in the now...all around this world of Yours, not just the ones here in this time and place. Make them all one as You, Father, are in Me, and I in You. Integrate them as You and I are integrated – unified, in harmony, inseparable.

22. "I have actually given them the glory that You gave Me, so that it would be possible for them to be one, even as We are.

23. "I have become one with them in the same way that You are one with Me, so that they may become completely one. This unification – this melding and merging of separate entities into a perfect oneness – is the thing that will ultimately show the whole world that You sent Me. They will all see that You love My followers as much as You love Me.

24. "Father, I truly want everyone You have given Me to be with Me...wherever I am...so that they will see, first-hand, the glory that You have given Me because You loved Me in the now...before the world of space and time was created.

25. "Righteous Father, the people of the world at large don't know the real You, but I know You, and now the ones who have followed Me know that You sent Me.

26. "And I have revealed You to them and will continue to reveal You through the coming manifestation of

the Holy Spirit. I am committed to continuing this revelation so that your love for Me may be in them and that I, Myself, may be in them, as well."

Chapter 18

1. When Jesus had finished speaking these words, He went out with His disciples over the Brook Kidron, across the Kidron Valley, to a place where there was a garden.

2. Jesus had often met there with His disciples, so they all knew where it was, including Judas.

3. So Judas came to the place with a whole battalion of soldiers and temple guards that had been sent by the Pharisees. They were all carrying torches or lanterns, and they were all armed.

4. But Jesus knew everything that was about to happen to Him, and He had no fear of it at this point. He had already made complete peace with His destiny. So when He saw the men, He calmly approached them and said, "Who are you looking for?"

5. "Jesus of Nazareth," they answered Him. But instead of responding to them by saying "I am He" or "That's Me," He just looked straight at the crowd and simply said the very same words God had spoken to Moses at the burning bush...He said, "I AM!"

6. And when He said those profoundly holy words, the sheer impact of them just knocked the entire battalion right off their feet, and they all went limp and fell backwards on the ground like dead men.

7. So then, having made it quite obvious by this act that no one was going to take Him by force, He calmly asked them again, "Now, who exactly did you say that you are looking for?" As soon as they were able, they jumped back up on their feet, shook off their shock, regained their composure and said, "Jesus of

Nazareth."

8. This time Jesus just said, "You are looking for Me; let these other ones go."

9. In saying that, He fulfilled what He had just prayed when He said, "I have not lost a single one of those you gave Me."

10. Then Peter, in his typical reactionary way, drew a sword and tried to kill one of the high priest's servants. But as he swung his sword, he was only able to slash off the right ear of one of them named Malchus.

11. But Jesus shouted at Peter, "What do you think you're doing? Don't you know that I am fully prepared to drink this cup that the Father is serving Me? Put your sword away!"

12. Then the entire detachment of troops, along with the captain and the officers of the religious leaders, arrested Jesus and tied Him up.

13. And immediately they led Him away to Annas, the father-in-law of Caiaphas who was serving as that year's high priest.

14. Caiaphas was the one who had advised the Jewish leaders that it was to their advantage that one man die for the people.

15. And Simon Peter followed Jesus on the way, along with another disciple who was acquainted with the high priest. So when they got there, the disciple with the connections went right into the high priest's court.

16. But Peter had to wait outside by the door until the other disciple could speak about him to the girl who was on duty. Then that disciple gained permission from her to bring Peter inside.

17. And when the girl came to let Peter in, she asked him as he entered, "Aren't you a follower of that man?" But Peter answered, emphatically, "No, I am not!"

18. Now it was a cold night, so several of the servants and temple police had built a charcoal fire and were

warming themselves by it.

19. Meanwhile, the high priest began interrogating Jesus about His followers and about His teaching.

20. But Jesus said to Him, "I have never conducted any underground meetings. Anything that I have said, I have said publicly – in the temple, out in the open, in all the usual meeting places.

21. "So why are you questioning Me? Just ask anyone who has heard Me, because they all know exactly what I have said."

22. As soon as Jesus said this, one of the temple guards stepped up and slapped Him hard across the face, shouting, "That's no way to talk to the high priest!"

23. Jesus looked at him and said, "If I have done or said something wrong, just say so. But if not, why did you slap Me?"

24. Jesus was still tied up, and Annas sent Him to the high priest, Caiaphas.

25. And while Peter still stood warming himself by the fire, someone else asked him, "Aren't you one of Jesus' followers?" And again, Peter strongly denied it, saying, "No, I certainly am not!"

26. Then, one of the high priest's servants there, who was also a relative of the man whose ear Peter had cut off, said, "Wait a minute; didn't I see you in the garden with that man? Yes, I'm sure that it was you and that you are connected to Him!"

27. Once again Peter denied it, but on this third time, while he was still speaking, a rooster outside the courtyard began to crow loudly.

28. Then they led Jesus from Caiaphas into the Praetorium (Pilate's official place of residence in the palace), just as the dawn was beginning to break. But they themselves did not enter the Praetorium so that they would not be defiled and could still eat the Passover later.

29. So Pilate went out to meet them and inquired, "What

accusation do you bring against this man?"

30. They answered him, "If He were not a criminal, a truly evil man, we would not have considered it so urgent that we bring Him to you."

31. Then Pilate said to them, "Whatever He has done that you think is so bad is really no concern of mine. Just take Him and judge Him according to your law, and whatever you decide to do with Him is fine with me." "But we no longer have the legal right to put a man to death," the people objected. "Only you Romans have the authority to perform executions now."

32. And so, what Jesus had predicted about His own death was about to come to pass.

33. Then Pilate went back inside the palace, called Jesus over to him and asked, "Yes or no...are you the King of the Jews?"

34. Jesus replied, "Is this your own, original question, or are you asking on behalf of someone else who told you about Me?"

35. Pilate answered, "I'm not a Jew! I have no knowledge or opinion of You. Your own people, including the chief priests, have brought You here, and I am simply curious as to the reason why. What have You done that has caused all this drama?"

36. Jesus answered, "My kingdom is not bound to this dimension. If it belonged to this world-system, My followers would not have handed Me over to the Jewish leaders. But it is not of this world, at least not yet."

37. "So You do say that You are a king," Pilate replied. Jesus answered, "Those are your words, not Mine, but, yes, I am a king – maybe not by your definition, but a king, nonetheless. I was born into this world to become the king over all truth, and everyone who is of the truth becomes a subject in My kingdom."

38. Pilate asked Jesus, "What is truth?" But Jesus at this point had nothing more to say to him. So Pilate went

back out and said, "Look, I just don't believe this man is legitimately guilty of anything!

39. "And since you have a custom that I should release someone to you at Passover, why don't you just allow me to release to you the "King of the Jews" and we'll be done with this business?"

40. But this idea only served to enrage them, so they shouted back, "No! Not this man! If you're going to release someone to us, then give us Barabbas!" Now Barabbas was a known terrorist.

Chapter 19

1. Then Pilate gave orders for Jesus to be beaten thirty-nine times with a whip made up of many lead-tipped leather thongs.

2. And the soldiers made a big, spiky crown of long, sharp thorns and pushed it down hard on His head. It painfully scraped through His scalp, causing scores of little bloody rivers to begin flowing into His eyes. Then, to humiliate Him further, they threw a royal purple robe across His shoulders.

3. "Hail! King of the Jews!" they sarcastically mocked, and when they did, a sort of maniacal fury broke out among the hundreds of men there and they all began to take turns punching Him in the face, as hard as they could, with their fists.

4. Eventually, Pilate, assuming that this violent episode with the soldiers would satisfy the people, went outside again and said to them, "I am going to bring Him out to you now, but you should know that I absolutely find Him guilty of nothing. But just the same, He has been severely beaten to satisfy you."

5. Then Jesus stumbled out before them, wearing the thorny crown that was now lodged into the top of His bleeding head. He was also wearing the once purple

robe that was now nearly completely crimson, having been saturated by the blood from several hundred deep lacerations around His body. And Pilate, dramatically gesturing with his hand to suggest closure to this whole, horrible scenario, said, "Behold! Here is the Man!"

6.   But when the chief priests and temple police saw Him in this condition – bleeding profusely, eyes swollen shut from the severe pummeling that He had received to His face – it only incited them to call for more blood. They yelled, "Crucify Him! Nail Him to a cross! Crucify Him until He is dead!" Taken aback and somewhat sickened by their savagery, Pilate said to them, "You crucify Him! I find Him not guilty."

7.   But the religious leaders replied, "By our laws He ought to die because He called Himself the Son of God."

8.   This merciless insistence for the execution of a seemingly harmless man terrified Pilate.

9.   So he re-entered the Praetorium, taking Jesus in with him. Inside, trying to understand the real situation at hand, he said to Jesus, "Where did You come from?" But Jesus did not answer him. He just stood there in silence, as the blood began to congeal all over His abused body.

10.   Pilate asked, "Why won't You answer me? Don't You realize that I am trying to save Your life? I alone have the power to let You go free or to nail You to a cross until You are dead. Right now, I'm the only friend You have in this world, so You need to start talking to me."

11.   Jesus then said to him, "You have no authority over Me or My life. Whatever power you may have in this situation is just what God has given to you, so don't be afraid to do what you have to do. Besides, the one who handed Me over to you did something worse than anything you can do."

12. At this point, Pilate determined in his mind to just override the people and let Jesus go free. He had no desire to let this thing go any further. But the religious leaders told him, "If you let this man go, you will show yourself to be disloyal and unfriendly to Caesar, because anyone who claims to be king is an enemy to the Emperor and a rebel against Rome."

13. When they said this, Pilate brought Jesus out to them once again and sat down on the judgment seat – a bench on the platform known as the Stone Pavement, or "Gabbatha" in the Aramaic language.

14. It was about noon on the day before Passover. And Pilate said to the people there, "Here is your King!"

15. Once again they yelled, "Kill Him! Crucify Him! Nail Him to a cross until He is dead!" Pilate said, "Do you actually want me to crucify and kill your King?" But they yelled even more loudly, "The Emperor is our king! We have no king but Caesar!"

16. So, realizing that he was completely incapable of persuading the people to have mercy, he gave in and handed Jesus over to the executioners, who led Him away to commence with the crucifixion.

17. And, despite the fact that Jesus had been beaten beyond recognition, with open wounds and eyes full of blood, He carried His own heavy cross of rough wood across the shredded flesh of His back and shoulders. Without protest, He carried it all the way to a place known as "The Skull," so named because of a weird rock formation in the side of the hill that looked very much like an actual human skull.

18. And, there, Jesus had large spikes driven through where His hands connected with His wrists and through His feet and ankles. When He was securely nailed to the cross, it was set upright between two men who were also being crucified.

19. And Pilate ordered that the charge against Jesus be written on a board and nailed to the top of the cross.

It read in bold letters, "JESUS OF NAZARETH, THE KING OF THE JEWS," and was written in Hebrew, Latin and Greek.

20. Then many of the local Jewish people read this sign, for the place where Jesus was crucified was near the city, and the words were written in three languages.

21. So the chief priests went back to Pilate and said, "Why did you write that He is the King of the Jews? You should have written that He merely *claimed* to be the King of the Jews. We demand that you have that sign changed immediately."

22. But Pilate, being fed up with their obsessive hatred of Jesus said, "That's enough from you people about Him. Let it go. What has been written will not be changed."

23. Then the soldiers, after nailing Jesus to the cross, took His clothes and divided them into four parts, one for each of them. But the tunic that He wore as an outer garment was elegantly crafted from a single, seamless piece of cloth.

24. So they said to one another, "This is a fine garment; let's not tear it, but rather gamble to see who gets it." And this fulfilled the Scripture that recorded David's prophecy when he said, "They divided My garments among them, and for My robe they threw dice."

25. So that is what the soldiers did. But standing by Jesus' cross were His mother and her sister, Mary (the wife of Clopas), and Mary Magdalene.

26. When Jesus saw His mother standing there, and the disciple that He loved standing nearby, He said to His mother, "Great lady, this man is now your son!"

27. Then He said to the disciple, "My brother, this woman is now your mother!" And from that moment on, that disciple took her into his own home and loved and cared for her as if she were his own mother.

28. After taking care of this last detail, Jesus knew that His work in the earthly dimension was now finished.

And, as was prophesied in the Scriptures, He said, "I am thirsty." This thirst was the last human sensation that He felt before leaving the physical body.

29. And a jar of cheap, sour wine was there, so someone in the crowd soaked a sponge with it and held it up to Jesus' mouth on the stem of a hyssop plant.

30. So when Jesus received whatever He could of the sour wine, He said, "Everything is done now; it is completely finished!" And, bowing His head, He simply released His spirit.

31. Now, because the next day would be the Sabbath and especially because it was Passover, the local people did not want dying bodies up on crosses during their special day. So they asked Pilate to have the men's legs broken to expedite their deaths, and to have their bodies taken down.

32. So the soldiers came and broke the legs of the other two men on either side of Jesus who were already nearly dead.

33. But when they approached Jesus, it was obvious to them that He had died, so they did not break His legs.

34. But one of the soldiers pierced His side with a spear and, when he did, a fountain of blood and water gushed out of the opening.

35. And the disciple who recorded all of this saw it first hand and testifies that it is all true; not one bit of it is hearsay.

36. These last two things were the further fulfillment of prophetic Scripture, for it is written, "Not a bone of Him shall be broken."

37. And in another place it says, "They will see the One in whose side they plunged a spear."

38. Joseph of Arimathea was a disciple of Jesus, but he had kept that fact a secret because he was afraid of the religious leaders. But now that Jesus was gone, he asked Pilate to grant him custody of His corpse, and Pilate gave him permission to take it down from the

cross, which he did.

39. Nicodemus (the same Nicodemus who had come to Jesus by night) then came with about seventy-five pounds of spices made from myrrh and various aloes.

40. And the two men wrapped the body in linen cloths with the spices, following the traditional Jewish burial custom.

41. And right in the same place where Jesus had been nailed to a cross, there was a garden with an unused tomb.

42. And so, because it was the customary day of preparation before the Passover and since the tomb was conveniently close at hand, they laid Jesus' body there.

Chapter 20

1. Early on Sunday morning, while it was still dark, Mary Magdalene came to the tomb and was surprised to find that the stone that had been lodged into the entrance had somehow been rolled away.

2. As soon as she assessed the situation, she immediately ran to find Simon Peter and the other disciple whom Jesus loved, and when she got to them she blurted out, "They have taken the Lord out of the tomb and we don't know where they have put Him!"

3. When Peter and the other disciple heard this, they just took off running to the tomb to see for themselves.

4. The two disciples initially were running together, but then the other disciple picked up speed and outran Peter, arriving at the tomb first.

5. And when he got there, he stooped down to look inside and saw the linen grave clothes lying there, but he didn't enter the tomb.

6. But when Peter got there, he just went right in and also saw the little pile of linen material lying there.

7.   Next to it was the piece of cloth that had been used to cover Jesus' face, neatly rolled up and in a place by itself.

8.   The disciple who got there first then entered the tomb and, when he saw the whole scenario, he believed fully in the resurrection.

9.   For, as yet, the disciples had not made the connection that the Scriptures had said that He would rise from the dead.

10. But even though he believed, the disciple didn't know what to do about it, so he and Peter both just went back to their homes.

11. Mary Magdalene, on the other hand, remained there and just stood outside the tomb weeping. And at a certain point, while she was still in tears, she stooped down and looked into the interior.

12. Inside, she saw two men who appeared to be angels, all dressed in white, sitting where Jesus' body had been. One was sitting at the head, the other at the foot.

13. They turned and looked right at her and asked, "Why are you crying?" She answered, "Because they have taken away my Lord's body, and I don't know where they have put Him."

14. As soon as Mary said this, she became aware that someone was standing right behind her. So she quickly turned around and saw Jesus standing there, but she didn't realize that it was Him.

15. Jesus asked her "Why are you crying, Ma'am? Who are you looking for?" She just assumed He was the gardener and said, "Sir, if you have removed His body, please tell me so that I can go and get it."

16. Then Jesus said to her, "Mary!" Suddenly, the sound of His voice penetrated her stupor and, realizing who He was, she cried out, "Teacher!"

17. When she reached out to embrace Him, He told her, "Don't try to hold on to Me, Mary. I am making the

transition into the Father's dimension, and you can't keep Me here. I no longer belong in the physical body that you are used to seeing and holding, so don't touch Me. But tell My disciples that I am going to our Father and to our God."

18. So Mary Magdalene went immediately to the disciples and declared to them that she had seen the Lord. She also told them what He had said to her.

19. But the disciples were afraid of the religious leaders, so, on the evening of that same day, they assembled themselves and barricaded the doors of their meeting room. But as soon as they built the barricade, Jesus just appeared in the middle of the room and said to them, "Peace be with all of you!"

20. When He had said this, He showed them all His hands and His side and, when they got over the shock of seeing Him, they became exuberant and began rejoicing.

21. Once again He said to them, "Peace be to all of you; just as the Father sent Me into this dimension, now I am sending you to all the people of world."

22. Then He took a deep breath and began to breathe and blow on them, and into them, in the same way that God had breathed into Adam in the creation. As He continued to blow on them, He began to say, "Receive…receive…receive the Holy Spirit.

23. "Receive the power to forgive sins; if you forgive the sins of any, they are forgiven; if you refuse to forgive them, they are unforgiven. You now have the same power and authority on the earth that I have had, not just to heal diseases, but to forgive sins, as well."

24. Now Thomas (called the Twin) was one of the twelve, but he was not with them in the room that night.

25. So when the disciples recounted to him the story of Jesus' amazing appearance and the transfer of anointing that took place there with them all, he was

more than a little skeptical. When they told him that they had seen the Lord, Thomas said, "Unless I see the holes in His hands made from the spikes and put my finger through them and put my hand into the opening in His side made by the spear, I will not believe."

26. So, a full week later the disciples were all together again, this time with Thomas, with the doors barricaded just like before. And in the same way, Jesus appeared in the middle of the room and said, "Peace be to all of you!"

27. Then He looked at Thomas, held up His hands in front of Him and said, "Go ahead, Thomas, put your finger through the holes in My hands and reach into the open place in My side. I don't want you to be an unbeliever, so if this is what it takes to get you to believe, then please explore all of My wounds; see for yourself and believe!"

28. But Thomas didn't have to touch Him. He knew immediately that it was Him and simply said, "My Lord and my God."

29. Jesus said to him, "Thomas, because you have seen Me with your natural eyes, you have believed. But there is a special blessing for those who have the faith, the vision, the imagination, to believe in what they can't see."

30. Jesus actually did many other miraculous signs in the presence of His disciples, miracles that are not even recorded in this book.

31. But the ones that are recorded here are written that you, the reader, may believe that Jesus was and is the Christ, the Son of God, and that, by believing in Him, you may live your life to the fullest in His name.

Chapter 21

1. After this, Jesus appeared again to His disciples, this time at Lake Tiberias (also known as the Sea of Galilee).

2. And this is how it happened: Simon Peter, Thomas (called "The Twin"), Nathaniel (from Cana in Galilee), and the brother of James and John were all there, together with two other disciples.

3. They were all still in a sort of subdued state of shock over everything that had happened in the last several days, and nobody knew what to do...how to act...how to live. Now that Jesus was gone, should they just go back to doing whatever they were doing before He interrupted their lives? He really hadn't been that specific in His instructions about what they should do post-resurrection. So Peter looked at all of them just standing around and said, "Well, I've got to do something! Life has to go on; I'm going fishing." And the rest of them, relieved that someone had finally broken the awkward silence and had come up with a plan, said, "We'll come, too!" So they all piled into the boat and started fishing, finding comfort in the normalcy of a familiar activity. And they fished all night long, but nobody caught a thing.

4. Early the next morning, Jesus stood on the shore, but the disciples did not recognize Him or realize who He was.

5. So Jesus called out to them, "Hey guys, have you caught anything?" And they answered Him with a simple, indifferent, "No."

6. Then He said, "Throw out your net on the right side of the boat and you will catch plenty of fish!" After staring blankly at Him for a minute, they all looked at each other and said, "Why not? What have we got to lose?" So they did what He said and almost

immediately began catching so many fish that they couldn't even draw the net back into the boat.

7. Then the disciple whom Jesus loved said to Peter, "You know who that is, don't you? It is the Lord!" When Peter heard this, he scrambled to put all his clothes back on and spontaneously plunged into the water, swimming as fast as he could to the shore. His immediate response to the thought of seeing Jesus was sheer elation; all he could think about was getting to Him, so much so that he forgot the fact they had not faced each other alone since the three denials.

8. The others stayed with the boat and tried to drag the overloaded net to the shore, for they were only out about three hundred feet.

9. When they got up on the beach, they saw that a charcoal fire was burning and fish was frying over it. There was also bread there to go with it.

10. "Bring up some of the fish that you've just caught," Jesus said.

11. So Simon Peter ran back to the boat and dragged the net to shore. There were one hundred fifty three large fish in it, but somehow the net didn't rip.

12. So Jesus Himself cooked breakfast for His friends and, when it was ready, He said, "Come on and eat!" But none of His disciples dared ask why He was there cooking for them, and they didn't have to ask who He was, because they all knew that it was Him.

13. Then Jesus took the bread in His hands and gave some of it to His disciples and then He did the same with the fish.

14. This was now the third time that Jesus had appeared to the disciples...the third time that He had shown Himself alive to them since being raised from the dead.

15. When they all had finished eating, Jesus turned and looked directly into Peter's eyes and said, deliberately, "Simon, son of John, I want to know if

you love Me more than the others do." Immediately, Peter's heart began beating faster because of the direct and serious tone in Jesus' voice. But he swallowed hard and, trying to sound as brave and as positive as he could, said, "Yes, Lord, You know that I love You!" Jesus replied, "Then feed My lambs."

16. Jesus then asked a second time, "Simon, son of John, do you love Me?" At these words Peter's heart was pounding so hard that he could feel his heartbeat in his temples. He began to tremble inside and with a softer, shakier voice said, "Yes, Lord, You know I love You." Jesus said, "Then take care of My sheep."

17. Then Jesus asked a third time, "Simon, son of John, do you really love Me?" At this third question, Peter just dropped his head and stared down at the ground. He could feel the sting of tears in his nostrils and his eyes began to well up. He knew what this confrontation was about – these three questions had to do with his three denials, but it was about more than that. This was about him being restored to the ministry – about being entrusted with the responsibility of feeding Jesus' beloved sheep – after doing something that should have disqualified him from ever having that privilege again. And, on its most basic level, this was about a friend being reconciled to a friend...about the Man-Jesus somehow needing closure from a personal hurt before He could move into the next dimension of His divine reign. Peter was deeply pained that Jesus asked him this question three times and, with tears streaming down his face, he said even more softly, "Lord, You know everything. You know that I love You." Jesus said, "Then I want you to feed My sheep."

18. He went on to say, "The truth is, when you were young, you were able to do as you liked. You were able to dress yourself and go wherever you wanted to go. But when you are old, you will stretch out your

hands because you will need others to dress and direct you, and they will take you where you don't want to go."

19. Jesus said this to tell Peter how he would be in his old age and how his eventual death would glorify God. Then He said to Peter, "Follow Me!"

20. Immediately Peter dried his tears and looked right over at the disciple who was perceived by everyone to be Jesus' favorite – the one who leaned on Jesus at supper and asked who was going to betray Him – and the competitive spirit rose up in him, triggering his old rivalry with this disciple. Instantly, his emotional mood changed. It didn't occur to him to question Jesus about this bleak prophecy that He had just spoken over him or to protest it in any way. All he could think about was what Jesus would say to the other disciple.

21. So Peter said to Jesus, "Wait a minute…what about him? What's going to happen to him in the future?"

22. Jesus answered him, "What is it to you? If I want him to remain alive on the earth until I come again, that is none of your concern. You just follow Me."

23. And so it seemed that Jesus pronounced the prophecy over Peter just to force a reaction out of him...just to cause his feelings of resentment toward the other disciple to rise to the surface so that they could be dealt with. In this way, Peter could be freed from this petty contention and move on to the important business of feeding Jesus' sheep. But then a rumor spread among the disciples that Jesus had said that *that* disciple would not die, which is not what He said, at all. The disciples desperately needed the Holy Spirit to come, because they were still misinterpreting Jesus' words, even after the resurrection.

24. And this is that disciple who saw all of these events, first hand, and has personally recorded them here. All of us who actually lived this story know for a fact that

this account of it is accurate, and now those who read it down through the ages will know that it is the truth, as well.

25. And Jesus actually did many other things that are not even recorded in this work, or in any other book for that matter. In fact, He was so prolific and innovative in His earthly incarnation that, if every ground-breaking thing that He did and said were recorded in detail, I imagine that the entire world could not contain all the volumes that would have to be written to cover the entirety of His amazing story! That's why His biography continues to be written through the vibrant lives of those who continue to follow Him...His story is still being written in the now!

Other books by Bishop Swilley . . .

Twenty-Three

New Reflections on the 23rd Psalm and You

The beautifully simple lyrics to David's timeless masterpiece remain as life-affirming and culturally relevant today as they were thousands of years ago when he originally wrote them. In this accessible, topical devotional based on his song that we know as the 23rd Psalm, you will find a positive "now" word for your every situation. You will want to keep a copy handy at all times to remind you that you can live fearlessly, even when walking through your own valley of the shadow of death. And when you are stressed out or feeling intimidated by those who try to oppose you, you will find in these pages the grace to help you lie down in green pastures and the encouragement to eat at the very table that the Shepherd has prepared for you in the presence of your enemies. His rod and His staff will comfort you at all times, and *Twenty-Three* will help you to use that road and staff more effectively and to enjoy a more fulfilling life as you learn to dwell in the house of the Lord forever.

From the Foreword: *"I wholeheartedly endorse both this book and the author. You will be encouraged, edified and uplifted with nothing but the good news. Bishop Swilley is a breath of fresh air in the religious climate of pretentiousness and egotism."*

-- Bishop David Huskins

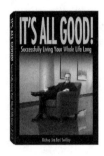

It's All Good

Successfully Living Your *Whole* Life Long

Pursuing peace with your *past* . . .
Perceiving purpose in your *present* . . .
Fearlessly facing your *future* . . .

All these themes *and more* are explored in this provocative study of the powerful implications of Romans 8:28 –

> *And we know that all things work together for good to those who love God, to those who are the called according to His purpose.*

Balancing the *secular* with the *sacred*, this candidly autobiographical and brutally honest book will make you *laugh* and make you *think*.

More importantly, it well help you begin to see how the plan for your life is unfolding every day and how God's "big picture" is revealing your destiny.

Every page contains good news and vital information about how to successfully live your **whole** **life** **long**. It's all here, and *it's all good!*

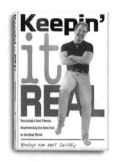

Keepin' It Real

Becoming a Real Person,
Experiencing the Real God,
in the Real World

You've never read a book quite like *Keepin' It Real!* In its pages, Bishop Swilley candidly examines an unusually wide array of subjects: the reality TV phenomenon...pop culture...history... politics...self-esteem...prosperity...success...parenting...multiculturalism...New Age philosophy...world religions...political correctness...racism...sexism...tolerance...activism...technology... addiction...eschatology...dispensationalism...the antichrist... orthodoxy...prayer...the Holy Spirit...destiny...purpose...vision... and much more, and addresses how they all relate to the Kingdom of God in the now!

But *Keepin' it Real* is also about *you* and how you can develop the courage and confidence to be yourself at all times and to live your *real* life without compromise. Socially relevant, thought-provoking, and theologically edgy, *Keepin' it Real* is a modern manifesto for REAL PEOPLE EXPERIENCING THE REAL GOD IN THE REAL WORLD.®

If you're ready to get *real*, get this book!

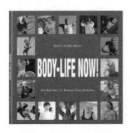

Body-Life Now!

Mini-Meditations for Maximum Fitness Motivation

Whether you're a serious body builder, competitive athlete, or just somebody who wants to drop a few pounds and be a little healthier than you are now, this power-devotional is for you! Inside you'll find 75 crisp little meditations on fitness, nutrition, attitude and lifestyle that will supercharge your workout and improve your outlook on your day.

You'll be doing yourself a big favor by incorporating these inspiring pages into your regular routine, *however* you choose to do so. Your spirit will be refreshed, your mind will be sharpened, and your body will thank you for the extra empowerment.

And if you're just getting *started* on the road to physical fitness, you'll find this book to be *especially* beneficial. It will serve as an easy-to-read road map for the journey designed to help you discover the new, improved *you.*

That journey can start right *here* . . . and it can start right *NOW!*

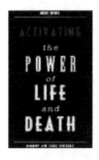

Activating the Power of Life and Death

It's Your Life . . .
It's Your Choice . . .
YOU CHOOSE!

God has given you the power to choose life or death, blessing or cursing. By the words of your mouth, you determine the quality of your life. This powerful book will help put you in charge of your life and future.

20/20 VISION

Changing Your Life
By Changing The Way You See Things

You can, in fact, change your life by changing the way that you see things. It has been theorized that there is no such thing as *reality*, there is only *perception* – a premise that can be argued, ad infinitum, by philosophers and physicists, alike. Whether or not it is actually and completely true, the fact remains that your perception of things really does determine how you think, feel and function every single day of your life.

You can determine your own happiness by learning how to properly view and discern the circumstances of your past and present. By learning how to see yourself correctly, you can become the person you've always really wanted to be or, better yet, you can reveal the best "you" that you already are.

What others have to say about *20/20 VISION*...

My friend, Bishop Jim Swilley, has written this masterpiece...and it is a sure invitation to a larger life by making that fundamental shift in your perception of reality. Let the words of this book give you the permission you need to open the windows of your perception, change the way you view yourself and the world you live in, and watch both you and that world undergo incredible and remarkable transformation!

Mark J. Chironna, PhD
Orlando, Florida

My friend, Jim Swilley, has successfully entered the marketplace of visualization and given correct spiritual understanding of a principle that literally creates success or failure, life or death, poverty or prosperity.

Prophet Kim Clement
Prophetic Image Expressions

Bishop Jim Swilley has taken the principles of Scripture and made them practical and doable. **20/20 VISION** *challenges its readers to elevate their perception from being downtrodden, victimized and hopeless, to be being empowered, capable and victorious.*

Bishop Eddie L. Long
Senior Pastor, New Birth Missionary Baptist Church

A Year In The Now!

a dynamic devotional dedicated to the daily discovery of destiny

Would you like to . . .

   . . . discover your destiny?
   . . . perceive your purpose?
   . . . validate your vision?
   . . . reinforce your relationships?
   . . . strengthen your self-esteem?
   . . . overcome your obstacles?
   . . . feed your faith?

You can . . . this year!
You can . . . by living in the now!
You can . . . one day at a time!

God is on your side! He is available to assist you in the pursuit of your potential as you develop the diligence to seriously search out your personal path for growth into greatness! Through seeking first His Kingdom and righteousness, you can become the person that He created you to be!

You can ONLY find God's Kingdom in the eternal NOW as you endeavor to experience Him in your everyday existence. Kingdom-seeking consists of a constant effort to embrace the now and a commitment to the continual conforming of your consciousness to it. This empowers and enables you to escape the mental distractions produced by living in the past or in the future, so that you can comprehend a real Christ for your current real circumstances!

A YEAR IN THE NOW! is a devotional designed to deliver a doable format for the daily development of your eternal life – to help you think creatively, beyond your familiar, time-bound comfort zones. These positive and powerful affirmations will provide the help you need to progressively put your life on the right track in realistic increments. You don't have to become overwhelmed by the tremendous task of trying to lead a *now life* in a *yesterday/ tomorrow world*. You can do it day by day!

This is your year to change your world! You can change your world by changing your mind! You can change your mind one day at a time! It's time for a fresh start, and you can start right NOW!

What others have to say about *A Year In The Now!*...

When my dear friend, Bishop Jim Swilley sent me a copy...I stopped everything I was doing and couldn't put it down...Jim is one of the most effective, prolific, and unique communicators I have ever met. He breaks down deep and profound truth and makes it palatable for all of us in such a practical way that just reading the principles and reciting the affirmations increases our life skills. The days are broken down into seven key principles a day, seven being the number of alignment between heaven and earth (4 being the number of earth, and three of heaven), whereby applying the seven daily truths your heart and mind are aligned with heaven's best and you are automatically brought into the kind of agreement that gets results in your life. If you want to get the "more" out of your daily life that has been promised to you in Christ I want to encourage you to get your hands on *A Year In The Now!* and make it a part of your daily spiritual discipline and focus.

Dr. Mark J. Chironna
The Master's Touch International Church

A Year in the Now! reads as a personal message to me. Each day I am encouraged – God is doing a new thing in the NOW...This devotional reinforces that God is working His plan in all things....

Germaine Copeland
Author of Prayers That Avail Much Family Books

Deeply profound, yet 'DO-ably' practical...Bishop Jim's 'easy to read' style of communication, combined with his witty grouping together of words that start with the same letter, define this devotional as a delightful way to delve deeper into your divine destiny as a daily discipline. Profound and practical, it's the perfect proponent to promote your personal progress.

Doug Fortune
Trumpet Call Ministry

A Year In The Now!...is extraordinary and powerful, giving day by day guidance on how to be strong in the Lord through seven pearls of wisdom each day. Seven! This is God's number for completeness and fulfillment. Through *A Year In The Now!*, God is truly using Bishop Swilley in a mighty way to unlock the wonderful mystery of the gospel so that each of us can live abundantly and serve God abundantly, in the now!

David Scott
United States Congressman, Georgia

About the Author

REAL PEOPLE experiencing the REAL GOD in the REAL WORLD®. This trademark of Church In The Now (CITN), founded in May, 1985 by Bishop Jim Swilley, is the theme of his entire ministry. A graduate of Southeastern University in Lakeland, Florida, he began preaching on the streets of Atlanta at age 13 and, since that time, has continued to do so throughout the United States and in many countries on five continents. He served for three years as the president of a branch of New Life Bible College, is a songwriter holding membership with ASCAP, has recorded multiple music projects, and is the author of nine books. In October of 1998, he was consecrated as a Bishop in the International Communion of Charismatic Churches (ICCC) and, in that capacity, provides oversight and covering to more than 170 churches and ministries.

Bishop Swilley is married to Debye, the Associate Pastor of CITN, and is the father of Jared, Christina, Judah and Jonah.

An audio version of *John In The Now*
(read by Bishop Swilley) is also available.

For more information on products
(or to inquire about large quantity purchases
for your ministry, church, or organization),
please visit our website at:
www.churchinthenow.org